AKC S.T.A.R. Puppy™

A Positive Behavioral Approach to Puppy Training

An Official Publication of the American Kennel Club

Mary R. Burch, PhD

Dogwise™ Publishing

Wenatchee, WA

AKC S.T.A.R. Puppy™
A Positive Behavioral Approach to Puppy Training
Mary R. Burch, PhD

Dogwise Publishing
A Division of Direct Book Service, Inc.
403 South Mission Street, Wenatchee, Washington 98801
509-663-9115, 1-800-776-2665
www.dogwisepublishing.com / info@dogwisepublishing.com

© 2013 American Kennel Club

Interior photographs: Mary Bloom except: Sheri Berliner (pages iii, 170), Mary Burch (pages 80 and 164) and Jim Leatherberry (pages 138, 141, 182 and 184).
Interior design: Lindsay Peternell
Cover design: Cuneo Creative, Tallahassee, FL.

ISBN 978-1-61781-097-8

Library of Congress Cataloging-in-Publication Data
Burch, Mary R.
  AKC S.T.A.R. puppy(r) : a positive behavioral approach to puppy training / Mary R. Burch.
     p. cm.
  "An Official Publication of the American Kennel Club."
  ISBN 978-1-61781-097-8
  1. Puppies--Training. 2. Puppies--Behavior. 3. Dogs--Training. 4. Dogs--Behavior. I. American Kennel Club. II. Title.
  SF431.B926 2013
  636.7'07--dc23
                                    2012023869
Printed in the U.S.A.

This book is dedicated to:

All of the AKC Canine Good Citizen Evaluators and instructors who help owners and their dogs have better lives together.

All of the dog owners who make the important commitment to train their dogs.

And most of all, this book is for the puppies. We're here for you.

Table of Contents

Acknowledgments

The American Kennel Club is pleased to acknowledge the following individuals who contributed to the writing and production of this book.

Mary R. Burch, PhD, is the Director of the AKC S.T.A.R. Puppy and Canine Good Citizen programs. Dr. Burch is an award winning writer and author of thirteen books, including *Citizen Canine*, which won the Dog Writer's Association of America award for the Best Training Book of the Year in 2010. Dr. Burch has trained dogs to the advanced levels of obedience, and she is a Certified Applied Animal Behaviorist and Board Certified Behavior Analyst (the human end of the leash). Dr. Burch is an AKC spokesperson and she is a frequent consultant in radio, television and print media.

Dennis B. Sprung is the President and CEO of the American Kennel Club. He has been responsible for many other AKC publications including *The AKC Complete Dog Book* and *AKC Dog Care and Training*. Mr. Sprung has been involved in the sport of dogs for more than forty-five years as a dog owner, breeder, exhibitor, judge, AKC Delegate, and president of an all-breed club. Mr. Sprung interacts with dog experts worldwide on important dog-related topics.

A picture is worth 1,000 words and we are indebted to award-winning photographer **Mary Bloom** for taking most of the photographs that bring this book to life. Additional photographs were taken by: **Sheri Berliner** (pages iii and 170), **Mary Burch** (pages 80 and 164) and **Jim Leatherberry** (pages 138, 141, 182 and 184). We would also like to express our gratitude to **Karen Reilly**, the **Port Chester Obedience Training Club (NY)**, and **Pat Tetrault** of Top Notch Dog Training for graciously permitting us to photograph puppy classes.

The following AKC staff members reviewed information in *AKC S.T.A.R. Puppy* related to their subject matter expertise:

- **Aliza Burns**
- **Michael Canalizo**
- **Curt Curtis**
- **Gina DiNardo**
- **Mary Donnelly**
- **Doug Ljungren**
- **Mari-Beth O'Neill**
- **Lisa Peterson**
- **Tom Sharp**
- **Daphna Straus**

Finally, a very special thank you goes to **Alan Slay**, **Bri Tesarz**, **Sharon Wilson** and **Susan Sanders** for the outstanding work they do supporting the AKC S.T.A.R. Puppy program.

Introduction

AKC S.T.A.R. Puppy: A Positive Behavioral Approach to Puppy Training
is the official guide to the AKC S.T.A.R. Puppy Program. The tagline
for AKC S.T.A.R. Puppy is that it is "the first step in training," and the
program is the puppy level of the Canine Good Citizen program.

Using scientifically validated behavioral methods, this book provides
how-to tips to demonstrate mastery of the twenty skills required
for earning the AKC S.T.A.R. Puppy certificate and medal. In order
to help prepare you to succeed in the program, the first part of the
book focuses on what we see as the four key elements of success:
socialization; training; activity; and responsible ownership. In addition, everything else a dog owner needs to know to raise a puppy
including practical information on developmental levels, crate training, housetraining, and suggestions for dealing with behavioral issues
is presented in this book. Each chapter presents skills in a way that
could be taught to young puppies, and a more advanced version for
older puppies is also included. Chapter 7 provides a list of exciting
AKC training activities and events in which all dogs can participate
after AKC S.T.A.R. Puppy.

Why is puppy training so important?

Puppies come into this world ready to learn. They arrive on this earth
pre-programmed to want to do the right thing when their needs are
met. There is perhaps nothing as innocent and honest as a newborn
puppy who trusts you and wants to please you. Puppies make us
laugh and feel happiness, joy and love, and we owe them a lot in
return.

One example of this pre-programming occurs when puppies are only four weeks old and are still stumbling around in a somewhat uncoordinated fashion. If kept in a clean whelping box of an adequate size, they will make their way to the far side of the box to relieve themselves…and then they wobble back to the side of the box in which they nap and spend time with the dam (the mother dog). This is the very first remarkable sign of pups wanting to stay clean and making an attempt on their own at the housetraining that will come later. The dam takes the responsibility for cleaning the puppies in the first weeks of life, but by four weeks, they begin to assist in this effort.

While a puppy comes equipped with a number of instincts that help him or her learn, breeders and new owners also have an important role to play early on. If the four-week-old puppies are in the hands of a responsible breeder who keeps the whelping box clean and begins taking the litter on regular, frequent trips outside, when those puppies go to new homes at eight weeks, if the same consistency and diligence is followed, it is possible to raise a puppy that rarely (or never) has a housetraining accident. However, if the new owner does not follow through with housetraining, problems will arise that can earn a dog a very quick one-way ticket to a shelter.

Where things go awry is when puppies have to fit into our harried human schedules that don't take the basic biological and social needs of a young canine into account. Not enough exercise, no opportunity to go outside for 'bathroom breaks' as often as needed for a young puppy, and no exposure at all to other dogs can result in a dog who started out perfect and problem free turning into a bit of a behavioral mess. And housetraining isn't the only issue—puppies who don't have the right experiences during the critical period of socialization will become fearful or possibly aggressive because they have not been taught over time how to interact with humans and other animals.

So while important, housetraining is not the only skill an owner needs to teach the new puppy. While some very experienced owners can train their own puppies, we believe that there are many benefits of working with a professional dog trainer while your puppy is still young. Dog trainers are becoming increasingly sophisticated with regard to skills related to helping dog owners who need guidance. Modern day trainers are learning about behavior analysis and operant conditioning, the science that can be used to solve behavior problems. We will review the best behavioral and training in Chapter 1 so you can take advantage of them as you work with a qualified trainer to help raise a problem-free puppy.

But, the science of applied behavior analysis and operant conditioning is not enough. Puppy instructors and new puppy owners need to understand the physical, biological and emotional needs of puppies. Play, exercise and socialization all play a critical role in transitioning the perfect puppy into adult dogdom with very few or no behavior problems. This is where the AKC S.T.A.R. Puppy Program comes in. AKC S.T.A.R. Puppy was created in order to help puppies and their owners work with experienced trainers to learn all the skills they need in order to succeed.

The AKC S.T.A.R Puppy Program: An overview

The AKC S.T.A.R. Puppy Program was developed by the American Kennel Club to help puppy owners, instructors, breeders, shelter staff and other canine professionals understand and meet the needs of this remarkable, extraordinary creature—the puppy. S.T.A.R. stands for **S**ocialization, **T**raining, **A**ctivity and a **R**esponsible owner, everything a puppy needs to have a good life.

Here's how it works. In the AKC S.T.A.R. Puppy Program, puppy owners and their dogs (up to one year old) attend a puppy class for at least six weeks. You'll go to class once a week for about an hour, and in between classes, practice with your puppy at home. In the last class, your instructor (who is an AKC Approved Canine Good Citizen Evaluator) will administer the twenty item non-competitive AKC S.T.A.R. Puppy test. Instructors may check off some of the test items sooner if your puppy completes them before the last class. Upon passing all twenty S.T.A.R. test items, you can complete the paperwork to have your puppy listed in the AKC S.T.A.R. Puppy records. You'll also receive a certificate from AKC, a monthly email newsletter and your puppy's beautiful gold AKC S.T.A.R. Puppy medal.

The AKC S.T.A.R. Puppy Program is administered by AKC Canine Good Citizen (CGC) evaluators. This is because AKC S.T.A.R. Puppy is actually the puppy level of the CGC program, and many S.T.A.R. puppies will transition from S.T.A.R. into CGC training. AKC Approved CGC evaluators are experienced dog trainers. They must meet several criteria including having a minimum of two years experience teaching people and their dogs in a professional or educational capacity. A training background that consists of just "I trained all of my own dogs since I was a child," or "I have been helping friends and relatives with their dogs," does not qualify one as a STAR/CGC evaluator. To find an AKC S.T.A.R. instructor near you, visit: http://www.akc.org/events/cgc/cgc_bystate.cfm

Raising a puppy right is hard work, it requires a lot of time and energy, and it certainly can be challenging. But raising a puppy is also one of life's greatest privileges. The AKC S.T.A.R. Puppy program will teach you how to get your puppy started on the right paw in life. When you provide your puppy with socialization, training, activities and you are a responsible owner, you'll build a bond with the puppy you love that will last a lifetime.

Chapter 1

What Makes a Puppy a S.T.A.R?

Think for a minute about the characteristics you would want to see in a puppy, whether that puppy belongs to you or is one that you encounter. Most people would probably list confidence, good manners, housetrained, healthy, friendly and happy on the list of desirable traits. On the other hand, a puppy that cowers with fear, barks incessantly, jumps up on you, destroys your possessions when you aren't looking or nips at your heels has behaviors that are not so desirable. We believe that there are four key elements that go into making a puppy a S.T.A.R.:

Socialization. Sometimes, when people consider getting a puppy, they think of training but they forget to think of the importance of socialization throughout the puppy's life. To socialize a puppy means to expose him to a wide variety of new things (including people, places and objects) in the environment. Socialization should continue throughout your dog's life, but you should work especially hard at socializing your puppy during his first three months of life. While a puppy comes readily equipped with plenty of instinctual behaviors, in many ways his young brain is like a blank slate ready to learn about life. Failure to be exposed at an early age to the kinds of things he will encounter later in life makes it much more difficult for a puppy to learn to cope with the world later on.

Training. For puppies, training goes hand in hand with socialization. Once the puppy has been fully exposed to his environment, he can be trained how to interact with people and other dogs. Training your puppy while he is young is much easier than trying to undo bad habits or overcome fears later in life. In training classes, you'll learn to teach your puppy basic commands that can be used to not only get your puppy to do something such as sit or stay, but the skills can also be used to manage behavior problems. For example, the "sit" command can be used to get your puppy to sit so you can brush her; "sit" can also be used when you want the puppy to do something other than jump on Grandma. Research shows that dogs who have been in training classes with their owners are less likely to end up in shelters due to behavior problems, and that a staggering percentage of shelter dogs have had no training. Training puts your puppy in a "learning to learn" mode and it strengthens the bond between you and your pup.

Activity. In AKC S.T.A.R. Puppy, when we say "activity" we mean both physical exercise and activities your pup can do with you. Dogs need daily exercise to stay both physically and mentally healthy. One of the worst mistakes a puppy owner can make is to acquire a high energy and intelligent dog and then not provide an outlet for the dog's physical and mental needs. Make sure you've done your homework and you know the level of activity your breed or mixed breed requires. In AKC S.T.A.R. Puppy classes, your instructor will look at your puppy's daily play and activity schedule. When a puppy is having behavior problems, if the activity schedule is modified, time and time again we see many of the behavioral issues disappearing.

Responsibility. Responsibility rests on you, the puppy's owner. Being a responsible owner means you will take care of your puppy's health needs, you will keep him safe by providing fences and using a leash where appropriate, and you'll provide your puppy with the training and activities he needs to have a quality life. Further, by never letting your dog infringe on the rights of others, you'll ensure that the rights of all dogs are protected. When dogs dirty hiking trails, parks and other public places, or run loose and scare non-dog lovers, the first reaction of many local government officials is to ban dogs from parks or trails. By being a responsible owner, you'll help ensure that dogs will remain welcome members of our communities.

Socialization

Socialization involves providing a puppy the opportunities to recognize and interact with other dogs, people, and in a broader sense, the environment. Puppies who are not well socialized can develop serious problems later in life that range from fearfulness to aggression. On one end of the continuum, dogs who were not well socialized as puppies might be extremely shy and fearful. At the extreme end of fearfulness, we see shy dogs who are afraid of new people, places, other animals and many things they may encounter in the environment. They may cower in the corner, shake and submissively urinate when a new person approaches, or they may be fear biters. On the other end of the continuum, puppies who have not had adequate socialization can also grow up to be dogs who are aggressive toward other animals and people.

A proper socialization process begins with the breeder carefully handling the puppies as newborns. By Week 3, puppies are then exposed to new people (who will happily volunteer to come and hold a puppy), new surfaces, sounds and other changes in the environment. A responsible breeder will have begun socializing your puppy before he comes to live with you. In fact, you should ask your breeder what has been done already to socialize your puppy and you should be wary of those breeders who don't provide you that information. If you get a puppy from a well run shelter, you can also expect that the shelter may have done some socializing. Unfortunately, many owners acquire a puppy at an age between eight and twelve weeks who has received only minimal socialization or none at all. If you find yourself in this situation, this means the burden of socializing will fall on you. However, if you follow the socialization tips found later in this chapter, you can help your puppy catch up.

Stages of development

The key to socializing a puppy is to know where the puppy is in terms of his stages of development at any given time so you can understand your dog's behavior. There is some variety in how behaviorists and dog trainers name and define developmental stages in puppies. While one book may organize stages into blocks of time by weeks and another by days, the information within each stage is usually similar. Further, some authors have created their own terms for specific developmental periods. Be aware that developmental periods are continuous and overlapping. Within a single litter raised under the same conditions, there may be variations in the progress of individual puppies.

In his landmark work, *Applied Dog Behavior and Training*, canine scholar Steven R. Lindsay lists four periods of development commonly recognized by most canine researchers:

1. **The neonatal period** (birth to 12 days).
2. **The transitional period** (12 to 21 days).
3. **The socialization period** (21 to 84 days).
4. **The juvenile period** (84 days through sexual maturity).

The neonatal period, birth to 12 days. The neonatal phase begins the day your puppy is born and is almost always completed by the time you meet your puppy.

The first contact most families will have with a new puppy will be when he comes home, generally at about eight weeks of age if acquired from a breeder, probably later if he is adopted from a shelter or rescue organization. If you're lucky, at least once in your life, you'll have the experience of observing very young puppies bred by a responsible breeder as they begin to develop during the first couple weeks of life. The dramatic changes in development in the first few weeks of your puppy's life are nothing short of miraculous.

While human babies take nine months from conception to birth, for puppies, the time is much faster. From the time of conception, a new litter is born 58 to 63 days later. For the first week after a litter of puppies is born, the job of the human caretaker is to provide warmth and shelter for the dam (mother dog) and litter and to take good care of the dam. From the time they are born until the second week of life, most puppies will double their body weight. The responsible breeder will begin to briefly handle the puppies so they become accustomed to touch and a change in position. The dam will take care of the dependent neonatal puppies by feeding, cleaning and watching over them. She'll keep them warm and lick them to stimulate bowel and bladder functions. Born with a sucking reflex in place, puppies will nurse to receive their mother's milk. They can taste, smell and feel touch, but when newborn puppies are born, they can't see or hear. There's not much action in the way of exciting canine behavior taking place in the first week of a pup's life. Nearly everything that is happening during this phase involves physical and neurological development.

The transitional period, 12 to 21 days. In the transitional period, the puppy transitions from the neonatal period which was marked by behavior that was mostly reflexive to voluntary, purposeful behavior. During Weeks 2 to 3, a puppy's senses start to develop and he will begin to react to a variety of stimuli. Your puppy will start hearing sounds and will move around in the litter to begin the very first, primitive, social interactions with the dam and littermates. The puppy will open his eyes about Week 2, and even though vision is not yet clear, the puppy will be able to recognize his dam and littermates. In Week 2, puppies begin to communicate their needs. They will cry when they are cold, hot or hungry. During the transitional period, puppies benefit from short periods of stimulation from a human. Holding the puppy and gently touching him builds the foundation for contact with humans. Between Weeks 2 and 3, the senses of vision, smell and hearing continue to improve.

The socialization period, 21 to 84 days. The care and handling that a puppy receives during the socialization period will influence his behavior for the rest of his life. Therefore, experts view this socialization period as the most important phase of canine development and divide it into two parts:

- **The primary socialization period, Weeks 3 to 5.**
- **The secondary socialization period, Weeks 6 to 12.**

Some experts define the "critical periods of socialization" as Weeks 3 to 5, and then again in Weeks 6 to 12. During Weeks 3 to 5, well socialized puppies learn skills that are critical to getting along with other dogs. During Weeks 6 to 12, puppies who are not well socialized are more likely to develop a variety of fears. More information on these critical periods will follow.

What is so critical?

A critical period of socialization means if the puppy does not receive the socialization and experiences necessary during this time, there is a good chance the puppy will have problems relating to people and other animals later in life. It is during these two time periods (Weeks 3 to 5 and again in Weeks 6 to 12) that a healthy emotional temperament is established.

By Week 3, puppies are interacting with objects and learning. Stability in the daily routine and environment is important as is continued time with the dam and littermates, however, as a method of sensory stimulation, new surfaces should be introduced (e.g., putting the puppy on a carpet and on a tile kitchen floor for a few minutes) as well as new people and sounds.

By Week 4, it will be clear the puppy is responding to auditory and visual stimuli in the world around him. The differences in individual personalities within the litter will begin to emerge; some puppies can be identified this early as pups who will grow up to be active dogs, while others are already showing signs of being quiet and mellow. The litter will be toddling around the whelping box, using unsteady little legs to crawl, stand, and attempt to walk and climb.

Puppies are still nursing during Week 4 when their tiny little needlelike teeth begin to emerge. It is at this point in time that puppies begin to learn bite inhibition, taught to them by the dam while they are still in the litter. There are also other important changes emerging with regard to the development of other behaviors and habits.

Bite inhibition

Bite inhibition is the process by which the puppy learns when a certain amount of force in a bite is not acceptable. If the puppy bites his mother too hard while nursing, she will yip and perhaps move away from the puppy (sorry pal, no more milk for you). In later weeks, both littermates and the dam will give feedback that a bite was too hard through yips, biting or ending a game. Thus the puppy learns to inhibit his bites. When puppies go to their new homes, the puppy owner teaches the next phase of bite inhibition, which is, "here's an acceptable chew toy—biting this is okay; biting me is not okay."

The dam begins teaching bite inhibition when the puppies are nursing. The lessons continue as pups play with the dam and littermates.

S.T.A.R. Story

"Years ago, I went every week to observe and take notes on a litter of Welsh Springer Spaniels bred by Dr. Rex and Toni Nowell. Weeks 1, 2 and 3 were interesting, but much of the time, I felt like I was watching little red and white hamsters as they slept. In the 4th week, all of a sudden, miraculously it seemed that the tiny, helpless neonatal beings had turned into puppies! They were busy moving around the large whelping box. Leaving their resting dam and siblings, the tiny pups would navigate their way on shaky little legs to the far side of the whelping box where they would relieve themselves. Even though I knew that puppies did this starting as early as three weeks of age, every time I observed a puppy making her way to the "bathroom area," I was astounded. At only four weeks old, puppies were going to a separate place rather than soil the area in which they slept and ate. I immediately saw huge implications for house training; puppies arrive in this world ready to be house trained and so many of the problems related to housetraining accidents are a result of how we, as humans, make mistakes." -Mary Burch

By Week 5, for most breeds, it's official! Even though she may still be living with a breeder, you've got yourself a puppy! Good luck with trying to take a good clear photo of a five-week-old puppy from a healthy litter. If you're holding her, she is likely to squirm and kick her feet as if to say, "Put me down, I'm very busy, I'm five weeks old and I have places to go!"

S.T.A.R. Story

"Hello AKC, what if I've fallen in love with a 2 year old shelter dog who was first found wandering in the county dump when she was a puppy—can she be a good dog for me?" AKC: The answer is clearly yes, but depending on the extent of neglect or lack of socialization, you may have a project on your hands and you might have to work harder with this dog.

By now, many breeders and puppy raisers will be transitioning puppies to water and puppy food. If they are teething, the puppies want to chew and bite. There is an increase during these weeks in active play and puppies are more social with humans. This is a good time to start separating puppies for short periods of time from their littermates so they can spend time with people who hold and play with them.

Puppies really begin to enjoy trips outside for fresh air, sunshine and fun. The running, jumping and wrestling with littermates and the tumbling that occurs now plays an important role in motor development, building coordination and strengthening muscles.

Even though puppies in this time period will start to show their independence as they run off to explore, the very beginnings of training can begin. Clapping your hands and saying in a cheerful voice, "Pup, pup, pup," will bring several puppies running to you with joy.

Running, jumping and tumbling build coordination.

Trips to the veterinarian during this time period provide an excellent opportunity for exposing the puppy to the sights and sounds in the big world outside the home. A car ride is an adventure in itself, and this is where the training can begin to teach the puppy to ride in a crate in the car.

At home, puppies are ready to tolerate an increase in noises and stimuli. The whelping box is no longer big enough for an active litter that now commands more real estate in the form of a room or play area designated by gates or an exercise pen. In addition to petting puppies and talking to them, grooming can begin with nail care. Most puppies will find more interest in toys and items they can mouth or carry around.

Your puppy should be exposed to many new stimuli and experiences.

While during the first critical period of socialization the emphasis should be on socialization with littermates and human members of the family, the emphasis during the secondary socialization period (Weeks 6 to 12) should be on exposing the puppy to new people. Dr. Ian Dunbar, the creator of the *Sirius Puppy Training* model, has a saying, "100 new people by 12 weeks." This is an excellent goal and one way to get your puppy to meet new people is to sign up for an AKC S.T.A.R. Puppy class. Puppy owners can also begin to work on socialization before classes start. See page 19 for "50 great socialization ideas."

A favorite socialization activity in AKC S.T.A.R. Puppy classes is called "Pass the Puppy." Dog owners sit on the floor and hold their puppies. When the instructor rings a bell, each puppy is passed to the person on the right. The puppies make their way around the circle and when class is over, they've got a lot of new friends!

The fear period, Weeks 6 to 12. During the first part of the secondary socialization period, approximately Weeks 6 to 7, there is a tendency for puppies to develop a fear of strangers so socialization at this time is critical. If socializing does not happen, some puppies can develop fearful reactions to stimuli such as loud noises, strangers and unexpected situations (e.g., a large man wearing a hat and a flapping rain coat approaches), usually between Weeks 8 to 12. When an owner reacts to a puppy's behavior (such as having a housetraining accident on the carpet) by yelling or screaming, the owner's relationship with the dog can also undergo serious damage. It is especially important in Weeks 8 to 12 to provide many positive, happy experiences for the puppy and to avoid traumatic events. In the case of puppies who have had a less than ideal start in life (such as shelter or rescue puppies), behavioral procedures such as systematic desensitization are useful in addressing fear related behaviors.

In Weeks 6-12, it is important to introduce your puppy to new people.

Social dominance period, Weeks 10 to 16. Researchers who have studied litters refer to the period from ten to sixteen weeks as the time that social dominance develops. But, the average puppy owner who gets a single puppy from a litter at eight weeks of age may not see social dominance in action. Social dominance begins with puppies in the litter competing for food. In multi-dog households, dogs often compete for food, resources such as toys, bones or a dog bed as well as owner attention. Social dominance is not the same thing as the now controversial "dominance theory" based on wolf packs.

The juvenile period (We hope it's not the juvenile delinquent period!)

The time from three months to sexual maturity is referred to as the juvenile period. From three to six months, puppies become increasingly independent.

S.T.A.R. Story

"I don't know what's up with my Chow puppy. The sweet little puppy that followed me everywhere and came running every time I called his name is acting like he has suddenly become selectively deaf. I say, 'Bear, Come!' What I see is Bear's rear end getting farther and farther away as he trots across the yard to do something that is apparently far more important than pay attention to me."

In the three to six months age range, using a leash is important. In AKC S.T.A.R. Puppy classes, you'll start to work on the recall, which means calling your dog to come to you. Recall training begins with the puppy on a leash, and progresses beyond AKC S.T.A.R. Puppy to the point that dogs will come to their owners when called from across the yard or the middle of a field.

Teething

Puppies get their first teeth at six to eight weeks. Then, when they are about three months old, they begin getting their permanent teeth and this process lasts until they are about eight months old. This is the time to lock up your favorite shoes. The chewing of objects by puppies should not be considered a behavior problem. Chewing is related to teething and is a natural part of development. Control the environment by puppy proofing your home and provide a rich assortment of acceptable chew toys.

If you get an older dog

When we say "puppy" most people visualize a puppy that is clearly a puppy—sharp little teeth, big round eyes and a dog who is in the age range of eight weeks to four months old. But, technically, dogs who are in the six to twelve month age range can be considered puppies and they too are welcome in AKC S.T.A.R. Puppy classes and should be thoroughly socialized.

Six to twelve months. Puppies in the six to twelve month age range are referred to as adolescents. They may be sexually mature, but often time pups in this age range are mentally like teenagers. Males become interested in females, and both males and females have hormonal changes and exhibit increased independence.

Males begin lifting their legs and they may spray your nice fabric sofa to tell other dogs, "this is MY house." Neutering will help eliminate scent marking. For all pet dogs who will not be shown in conformation dog shows, spaying or neutering is recommended.

In the six to twelve month age range, there can be a second time in the puppy's life when he develops fears to new people or situations. At any sign fearfulness is developing, the puppy needs more socialization and exposure to new people, places and things. Because dogs with behavior problems at this age are at risk for relinquishment to a shelter, after AKC S.T.A.R. Puppy, we recommend Canine Good Citizen training so that puppies (and their families) have continued support throughout this phase.

Looking forward to your puppy's future
The adult dog: twelve months to two years. At one to two years old, your sweet puppy has moved into the stage of being an adult dog. When trainers refer to "adult dogs," they generally mean the dogs are grown and sexually mature. Some breeds still act like puppies well into their second year and trainers may refer to them as "slow maturing."

The stage in your dog's life when he is a young adult is an exciting time for training because adults are ready for the action in formal training classes for agility, obedience, rally, field, and other exciting activities. To ensure that dogs have had a chance to mature, one year is the minimum age for most dogs to be tested and registered/certified by therapy dog organizations. For more info on therapy dogs, see www.akc.org/akctherapydog.

Hopefully, by now, both you and your dog have earned the Canine Good Citizen Award or you're training for the CGC test that marks you as a responsible owner and shows that your dog has basic good manners.

The adult dog: two to four years. If you've raised your dog since she was in AKC S.T.A.R. Puppy classes, by now you should have a great companion. Even though you've made it through housetraining and dealing with behavioral issues, socialization and exposure to new sights, sounds, and people should continue throughout your dog's life. Chapter 7 outlines the many fun AKC activities in which you and your canine companion can choose to participate either for fun or competitively.

The senior dog: six years and older. For nutritional purposes, dog food companies define the senior dog as six or seven years or older. However, there are some dramatic differences in the aging process that are related to size and breed. In general, very large dogs have a shorter life span, and thus, when they are six years old, they are indeed senior dogs. Smaller dogs may live as long as fifteen or sixteen years, so at six years old, they may appear to be in their prime and still be involved in training, athletic activities and competitive events.

As a matter of fact, in 2011, Ashley Deacon and his Pyrenean Shepherd Luka de La Brise (also know as "Luka") showed the world just what an older dog who is fit and healthy can do when the pair won the Gold Medal in the FCI Agility World Championship in Lievin, France on the weekend of Luka's ninth birthday.

There can be some health issues that are specific to older dogs. Certainly, as with people, when dogs age, they can develop health problems including specific diseases as well as vision, hearing, heart, bowel and bladder trouble.

There are also behavioral issues that can arise with senior dogs who never had a history of behavior problems including:

- separation issues
- aggression (to people and other animals)
- noise phobias (including storms)
- increased vocalizations (whining and barking)
- nocturnal restlessness
- housetraining issues
- non-compliance

Yet, despite challenges, living with an older dog can be one of life's greatest experiences. The bond that comes from living with a dog throughout his lifetime is like no other.

If your older dog is one that you have acquired as an adult or senior dog, you've been entrusted with the honor of assuring that the rest of this dog's days are filled with comfort, love and quality of life.

50 ideas for socializing your puppy

In the continuum of socialization with humans, puppies first learn to tolerate your presence, then meet people, greet/interact with people, tolerate people while interacting with them (holding, brushing), and then follow simple commands. First, your puppy should get to know you, then members of your family and visitors to your home and finally, the puppy should meet people out in the community. While we are focusing on puppies, if you acquire an older dog, even a senior dog, he or she would benefit from these socializing ideas.

Getting to know you

The first step in socialization is for your puppy to be comfortable around you.

You should be able to:

1. Pet your puppy.
2. Hold your puppy in different positions (pick up and hold small dogs).
3. Hold the puppy on your lap.
4. Handle your puppy (checking the mouth, ears included).
5. Play with the puppy.
6. Touch the puppy's feet.
7. Put a collar or harness on your puppy.
8. Walk your puppy on a leash fifteen steps.
9. Call the puppy to come.
10. Have the puppy perform a basic skill such as sit or down (use food to guide a young puppy).
11. Have the puppy perform a functional skill such as "get in the crate" or "go to your bed." You may use shorter verbal instructions such as "Crate," as you point into the crate.

Getting to know the family

After your puppy feels comfortable with you, family members should be able to:

12. Pet the puppy.

13. Hold the puppy in different positions.

14. Handle the puppy (checking the mouth, ears included as a veterinarian would do).

15. Play with the puppy.

16. Touch the puppy's feet.

17. Let a family member put on a collar or harness.

18. Walk the puppy 15 steps on a leash.

19. Call the puppy to come.

20. Have the puppy perform a basic skill such as sit or down (use food to guide a young puppy).

21. Have the puppy perform a functional skill such as "get in the crate" or "go to your bed." The family member may use shorter verbal instructions such as, "Crate," while pointing to the crate.

Getting to know visitors

If puppies are shy, it helps to introduce them to visitors who are sitting on the floor, or at a minimum, sitting down. It can be intimidating for a puppy to have someone standing over it.

22. Meet a visitor in the yard or outside (with the owner nearby if the puppy is uncertain).

23. Meet a visitor in the house with the owner nearby.

24. Allow petting by the visitor to the home (visitors should include adults, children, men, women, etc.).

25. Come to the visitor (in the house) when encouraged.

26. Take a treat from the visitor.

27. Play with a visitor (chase a ball, play with a toy).

28. Follow the visitor a short distance when playing.

29. Greet/interact with more than one visitor in the home.

30. Comes close to a group of visitors (company) in the home.

31. Meets company, allows petting.

Meeting friendly strangers

Your puppy should meet all kinds of people when out in the community. When you're introducing your puppy to all sizes, shapes and types of people, don't forget to do so in all kinds of new places. Playgrounds, lakes, local parks (don't get in a rut and go to the same park every day), walks in your neighborhood, walks in other neighborhoods, visiting your job if permitted, eating at an outdoor dog-friendly restaurant, and walking on leash at a shopping area are just a few of the places you and your pup can go to see people.

32. Meets a young boy.
33. Meets a young girl.
34. Meets a group of children.
35. Allows petting by children.
36. Walks with owner on a playground with noisy children.
37. Meets a male teenager.
38. Meets a female teenager.
39. Allows petting by a male teenager.
40. Allows petting by a female teenager.
41. Meets an adult male (include different appearances, body sizes, voices).
42. Meets an adult female (include different appearances, body sizes, voices).
43. Meets an elderly person.
44. Allows petting/handling by a veterinarian or veterinary technician.
45. Allows grooming (for younger puppies, this will be done at home).

With proper socialization, your puppy should tolerate gentle handling from a child.

This puppy has already learned to be calm when handled by a veterinarian.

Meets a person who is:

46. Wearing a hat.
47. Wearing a big coat.
48. Wearing sunglasses.
49. Using crutches or a cane.
50. In a wheelchair.

Introduce your puppy to new outdoor areas such as sidewalks, playgrounds and parks.

Training

In AKC S.T.A.R. Puppy classes, you'll learn a lot about training behaviors (such as sit, stay, down and come) as you work on the twenty items to earn the AKC S.T.A.R. Puppy award. For young puppies (who are two to four months old) in AKC S.T.A.R. Puppy classes, the emphasis in the class is on socialization, play and learning the very beginning of basic skills. Young puppies have shorter attention spans, therefore, it is not appropriate considering their developmental levels to require precision (e.g., perfect heeling on leash) and intensive or lengthy drills during training. Older puppies (closer to one year) who are just beginning training may progress more quickly through S.T.A.R. skills and learn Canine Good Citizen skills and other more advanced tasks. We recommend that all members of your family who live with the puppy attend the training classes.

AKC S.T.A.R. classes are for the whole family.

In AKC S.T.A.R. Puppy classes for young puppies, instructors tailor the instruction to meet the developmental needs of puppies. For younger puppies, most of the class in the beginning will be geared at play and socialization. By the time the puppies graduate six weeks later, they are developmentally ready to begin learning additional new skills.

Nature vs. nuture

Just as is the case with humans, even when you provide an ideal amount of socialization, some puppies will have natural tendencies to be "social butterflies" and others will remain more reserved. Some breeds of dogs have been bred for generations to be guard dogs while some have been bred to be lap dogs. However, no matter what your dog's personality, with proper training and ongoing socialization, you can ensure that your puppy will be free of aggression toward people.

It is important to note that when puppies begin class at eight weeks of age, the class does not look like a standard basic training class with a heavy emphasis on teaching "obedience" skills or performing drills on tasks such as heeling. Young puppies should be given a chance to play and learn functional behaviors such as "get in the crate" during S.T.A.R. classes.

Training should be based on sound principles

Different instructors may have a variety of techniques for training puppies, but basically what you should look for is a method that is based on sound scientific principles about how behavior works. Using a behavioral approach will result in not only you being an effective trainer, but you and your puppy will also develop a healthy relationship. Here are a few key concepts:

- **Reward behavior you like.** The best way to get a puppy to do something is to reward it, whether you wait for the behavior to happen, lure the pup with a treat into doing something, or by positioning the dog. Treats, toys and your attention make great rewards.

- **Use management to avoid problems.** Managing your puppy's environment to make it harder to do something 'wrong' is a great technique. A common example is to keep your curtains closed if your pup likes to bark at people walking by until you can train your dog to do something other than bark.

- **Teach incompatible behaviors to replace undesirable behaviors.** If your puppy has begun to jump up on people when greeting them, teach him to sit by giving him a treat every time he does so. A dog cannot sit and jump up at the same time. Trainers call this DRI, differential reinforcement of an incompatible behavior.

- **Don't inadvertently reinforce behaviors you don't like.** This is very common among both owners and people who meet your pup. Petting and playing with a dog who jumps up on you is a great way to ensure he will always jump up when greeting. Instead, ignore a puppy who seeks your attention when he jumps up on you, or better yet, prompt the puppy to sit and then pet him.

As mentioned above, we can't emphasize enough that socializing your puppy is a great way to make training a smooth process. A happy and confident puppy is much easier to train. Giving your dog lots of exercise and playing with him also helps with training. Training and exercise are the winning combination for a raising a dog who will be a joy to live with. **Dogs who are bored out of their minds create their own activities and a lot of times, those activities spell trouble.** Exercise results in a dog who can be calm when in the house—dog trainers have a saying, "A tired dog is a good dog." Training gives a dog something to wrap his mind around and the activity provided by practicing for and attending training class can benefit both you and your puppy.

The basics of behavior

When it comes to training animals or people, it helps to have a basic understanding of the science of behavior. Because modern day dog trainers are more sophisticated than ever when it comes to understanding canine behavior, you're likely to hear your trainer use terms such as reinforcement, clicker training and extinction as your dog is being taught the new skills covered in Chapters 5 and 6.

Let's take a few minutes for a behavioral review. In 1938, B. F. Skinner published a landmark scientific work, *Behavior of Organisms*. In this book, Skinner explored the link between animal's behavior, consequences and reinforcement. Simply put, if an animal or person does something and finds the consequences of it rewarding he will likely do it again. In the 1940's, behavioral researchers using Skinner's ideas began to train animals to do amazing things such as teaching pigeons to release bombs and large marine mammals to perform in entertainment shows. By the 1980's, Skinner's research was being applied successfully to dog training.

Operant conditioning

Operant conditioning is part of the science of behavior developed by Skinner that explains the functional relationship between environmental events and behavior. Operant conditioning explains how all animals, including people and puppies, learn. Examples of operant conditioning taking place are when:

- You successfully teach a puppy to sit using a food reward.
- You ignore a dog for begging at the table and he soon stops.
- A child continues to do math problems as a result of teacher praise.
- A worker avoids talking to a supervisor who is always grouchy and negative.
- A person who is gambling doesn't want to leave the slot machine because she wins every now and then (this is called a variable schedule of reinforcement).
- A driver who is speeding slows down when she sees a police car at the side of the road.

Operant conditioning has four main principles: 1) reinforcement; 2) extinction; 3) punishment; and 4) stimulus control.

Reinforcement

Reinforcement is when a behavior, followed by a consequent stimulus, is strengthened or becomes more likely to occur again.

A **stimulus** is any object or event that can be detected by the senses and can affect an animal's (or person's) behavior. For dogs, stimuli are sounds, food/water, smells, touches and visual signals. In training sessions, examples of stimuli that are used with puppies are verbal commands, encouraging noises and hand signals.

Reinforcement (or reinforcers) can be further broken down into several categories. These are: primary reinforcement; secondary reinforcement; positive reinforcement; and negative reinforcement.

Primary reinforcement. Primary reinforcers are those that are related to biology. Examples of primary reinforcers include food, drink, some kinds of touch and sexual contact. When you train your puppy using a food reward (contingent on the puppy doing what you wanted her to do), you are using a primary reinforcer. Sometimes trainers also use the word "reward" in place of reinforcer.

Secondary reinforcement. Secondary reinforcers are those that become reinforcing by being paired with primary reinforcers. Secondary reinforcers for humans have a social context. Examples of secondary reinforcers for people are money, praise, attention and smiles from others. For dogs, secondary reinforcers include praise, the sound of a clicker and clapping your hands. In clicker training, trainers pair praise, clicks, etc. with food rewards (primary reinforcers). The use of food can eventually be reduced since praise, pats and clapping become rewards themselves as a result of the systematic pairing.

Clicker training. Clickers are small metal and plastic devices that trainers hold and use to make a clicking sound. In clicker training, a dog is first given food alone as a primary reinforcer. Once it is clear the dog likes the food rewards and is responding to them, the clicker is clicked, then food is given. The clicking sound is thus paired with food, so the click begins to function as a reinforcer. Clickers are conditioned reinforcers because they start out as a neutral stimulus, meaning the initial noise has no meaning for the dog. Over time, by pairing the clicks with food, the dog learns that the sound of the clicker means, "Good boy!"

Positive reinforcement: Good things will come your way. A positive reinforcer is a stimulus that, when presented following a behavior, makes it more likely that the behavior will occur again in the future. When you're training your puppy, positive reinforcement can be either 1) primary reinforcers that you'll use such as food rewards; or 2) secondary reinforcers such as toys and praise.

Negative reinforcement: Escaping and avoiding unpleasant things. This is a tricky term because people hear the word 'negative' and think this involves doing something painful or unpleasant to the dog. It doesn't. Negative reinforcement is when the probability of a behavior occurring in the future is increased when the behavior is followed by the removal or avoidance of a negative stimulus. With positive reinforcement something is added (such as food, toys) and with negative reinforcement, a negative stimulus is removed to condition an avoidance response. In humans, putting on a coat to avoid being cold is an example of negative reinforcement. In dog training, when the training involves corrections and the dog works to avoid corrections (e.g., "NO!"), the principle involved is negative reinforcement.

Schedules of reinforcement: How often do I give my puppy a food reward when training? Schedules of reinforcement define which responses will be reinforced and how often they will be reinforced. Reinforcement can be continuous (in which every single instance of a desired behavior is reinforced) or it can be intermittent. Intermittent reinforcement means only some of the responses will be reinforced. For example, you could give your puppy a food reward every fourth time she did a desired behavior correctly. This is called a fixed ratio schedule of reinforcement. You could give her a reward every now and then on an unpredictable schedule of intermittent reinforcement. This is the schedule that maintains behavior the longest. This is why slot machines work; the person never knows when the slot will pay off, and thus, continues playing. A good basic book on operant conditioning can teach you about schedules of reinforcement.

Extinction
We've talked about using reinforcement to change behavior. Extinction is another operant (learned) conditioning method that can be used to change the behavior of people or animals.

Extinction can occur if a behavior that has been previously reinforced is no longer reinforced. Over time, the result will be that the behavior no longer occurs. Probably the best extinction example related to your puppy will be begging at the table. If your dog develops the habit of begging, it is because someone has reinforced the behavior by giving food to the dog who begs as the following anecdote illustrates:

One sweet grandmother who lived with a family told us, "I don't know why Duke begs so much. I only give him a bite from my plate every now and then." Good grief! She's put him on a variable schedule of reinforcement. He's playing the dinner table slot machine and having Grandma sneak him some pot roast "every now and then" results in the strongest schedule of reinforcement possible for the undesired behavior. Extinction will occur by completely withholding all of the reinforcers that are maintaining a behavior. For extinction to work with Duke, everyone in the family needs to ignore the inappropriate behavior and reinforce desired behaviors. The family could give Duke a treat for waiting nicely on his dog bed while the family enjoys their meal.

Punishment

The topic of punishment often comes up when people are talking about dog training. Like the sometimes confusing term "negative reinforcer," it would have been far less confusing if punishment had been called something else in operant conditioning.

In the science of operant conditioning, "punishment" is defined as providing consequences for a behavior that decrease the probability the behavior will occur in the future. In the scientific sense, even a brief "time out" for an unruly puppy is technically a punisher if it results in a decrease in behavior.

Unfortunately, in our culture, the term punishment conjures up images of children who are being punished by being sent to bed without their dinner. When it comes to dogs, people sometimes think of punishment as an owner being emotional, overly dominant or abusive when correcting a dog. Screaming at a dog, hitting him and shaking a newspaper are examples of inappropriate and abusive owner behaviors. They are neither humane or effective forms of punishment.

Dog training can involve a variety of punishment techniques including time outs, response costs, verbal reprimands, and both physical and natural punishments. With the exception of the harsher forms of physical punishers, these kinds of punishments can be both humane and effective.

Time out. Time out involves the withdrawal of attention. For a puppy who is out of control, sometimes a minute or two in a crate will help the puppy settle down.

Response cost. Response cost means withholding a reinforcer as a result of an undesired behavior. For children, a common response cost procedure is losing playground time for misbehaving in the classroom. For puppies, an example of response cost might be the removal of a toy.

Verbal reprimands. A verbal reprimand can sometimes be successful in stopping a behavior. Examples of verbal reprimands include "Aaah-hhh!!," "NO!" and "Stop that!"

Natural punishment. Sometimes the world provides a natural punisher. For humans, touching a hot stove will decrease the likelihood that you won't be doing that again in the near future. For dogs, an example of a natural punisher is when a dog puts his head in some bushes, comes out with a bee sting on his nose, and then wants no part of being near those bushes in the future.

Physical punishment. Remember that the purpose of this section is to explain operant conditioning terminology and that we are not suggesting all of these procedures be used when training your puppy. Examples of physical punishment include hitting a dog, leash corrections, or doing something such as kneeing it in the chest (to stop jumping). Good trainers can almost always find alternatives to physical punishment to stop unwanted behaviors.

Stimulus control

Behaviors are said to be under stimulus control when there is an increased probability that the behavior will occur as a result of the presence of a specific stimulus. With many dogs, if you shake your car keys or open the refrigerator door, they come running. The dog can quickly learn that the one means a car ride and the second means it is meal time. What stimulus control should mean for you when you're training your puppy is that you'll want to use the same motions, verbal cues and other physical cues when you are training so the dog knows what is expected.

Behavioral procedures and concepts

We explained the four basic principles of operant conditioning (reinforcement, extinction, punishment, and stimulus control). Related to those principles, there are a number of behavioral concepts and techniques which are now commonly used by dog trainers that you may encounter. While the terminology may be unfamiliar to you, by the time you have completed the AKC S.T.A.R. Puppy program, you will have employed many of these concepts and techniques with your puppy.

Counter-conditioning. This is a technique that is used with behavior problems such as fear and anxiety. *Counter-conditioning gets its name because it 'counters' the effects of earlier conditioning that was usually aversive.* Suppose a puppy has developed an intense fear of a vacuum cleaner. Starting with the vacuum cleaner turned off and at the other side of the room, the trainer could feed the puppy a preferred treat in the presence of the vacuum. The vacuum cleaner would slowly be moved closer while the puppy is fed treats until the puppy no longer showed fear because he now associates the vacuum cleaner with a pleasurable activity. Counter-conditioning is often used with dogs who don't like getting their nails clipped. Look for other examples of how to use this technique in Chapters 5 and 6.

Systematic desensitization. *Systematic desensitization is a form of counter-conditioning that uses a hierarchy of the least to the most problematic situation.* In the case above of the vacuum cleaner, the unplugged vacuum cleaner on the opposite side of the room twenty feet away is less threatening than a vacuum cleaner turned on and being pushed by the dog at a distance of three feet. Gradually moving the vacuum cleaner closer to the dog while feeding him is an example of counter-conditioning and systematic desensitization together.

Habituation. To understand habituation, think of repeated exposure. *Habituation is when the animal has less of a negative reaction to an event after being exposed to it several times.* Examples of this related to dogs are when sporting dogs get used to the sound of guns being shot, or therapy dogs who get accustomed to a busy, noisy day room in a rehabilitation facility.

Generalization. You may find that teaching your dog to sit in your living room is easy, but to do so in a park is hard. A dog who can sit on command *in a variety of environments is said to have generalized that behavior.* The ultimate goal in training your dog is that your dog can do the behaviors you've taught, anywhere, any time, with any person present. If your puppy will sit on command in your living room every single time you practice, but she won't sit in the backyard or at class, the training has not generalized yet and additional work is needed.

Schedules of reinforcement. Schedules of reinforcement are complex and there are a number of books that explain this concept in detail. Basically, *schedules of reinforcement define which responses will be reinforced and how often the behavior(s) will be reinforced.*

Continuous reinforcement. *When a behavior is reinforced every single time it occurs, it is called continuous reinforcement.* Continuous reinforcement is often used when beginning to teach a dog a new behavior. If you gave your pup a treat every time he sits, the puppy would be said to be on a continuous reinforcement schedule. While continuous reinforcement is a great technique for teaching a new skill, it should eventually be reduced to a more practical level.

Intermittent reinforcement. *Intermittent reinforcement is when responses are only reinforced some of the time.* Intermittent does not necessarily mean random. A **fixed ratio** means a behavior would be rewarded a specified number of times. A **variable ratio** means a behavior is rewarded in a random fashion.

Shaping. *Shaping is when successive approximations of a desired behavior are reinforced.* For example, if you wanted your puppy to walk on a low, stable board as early exposure to an agility task, you could reinforce the puppy for getting close to the board, putting one paw on it, standing on it, and then finally, for walking on the board. You will see that shaping is recommended in later chapters to teach your puppy more complete behaviors.

Chaining. *Chaining is when behaviors in a sequence are reinforced.* Have you ever seen an old Lassie show on television? Lassie runs across the room, jumps out a window, runs across the yard, and barks at the boy who has fallen in the well. That is an example of a behavioral chain. And actually, for the record, there never was a show where Lassie found a boy who had fallen in a well. Canine Freestyle dogs who learn a dance have been taught through chaining and the obedience Utility exercise called the go-out where the dog runs away from the handler, turns, sits, and then goes over a jump is a chain.

Fading. *Fading is when the strength of a prompt is gradually reduced.* In training your puppy, if you fade a verbal command to a whisper and then to a hand signal only, you're using fading. As you progress from walking your dog on-leash to off-leash, you've used fading. Use of food treats can usually be faded for most behaviors but a treat now and then can keep your dog motivated. In Chapter 6, you will see how to fade rewards and verbal praise.

When should you start training? The answer may surprise you

It used to be that trainers and veterinarians recommended that puppies delay training classes until they were old enough to have all of their vaccines and boosters. What this meant was that some puppies didn't get to class until they were four to six months of age. By this time some had already developed behavioral issues and were headed down the path to a problem that started in the Critical Period of Socialization or Fear Period.

As a result, many veterinarians, veterinary technicians, animal behaviorists and trainers now recommend that puppies (who do not have health issues) begin classes as early as seven to eight weeks. The American Veterinary Society of Animal Behavior (AVSAB) states: *"In general, puppies can start socialization classes as early as 7-8 weeks of age. Puppies should receive a minimum of one set of vaccines at least 7 days prior to the first class and a first de-worming. They should be kept up to date on all vaccines throughout the class."* Waiting too long to begin classes can result in inadequate socialization during the first two to three months of the puppy's life and result in behavioral issues (including fears, phobias, avoidance and aggression) that extend well into the dog's life. For the complete statement, see: *http://www.avsabonline.org/avsabonline/images/stories/Position_Statements/puppy%20socialization.pdf.*

If you are working with a mentor who advises you not to begin classes until your puppy is older, make sure you have a plan in place for socializing your puppy.

S.T.A.R. Story

"My AKC S.T.A.R. Puppy classes have always had a waiting list. The STAR class is my favorite one to teach and I can see a difference when puppies begin training early. The transition to Canine Good Citizen is very natural for puppies who have been through STAR training and many of my students go on to train and compete in other activities such agility, rally, and obedience. So that puppies and their owners don't have to wait weeks for the next round of classes to begin, I now use a module approach so that training can start as soon as an owner has the puppy. I educate students about the importance of vaccines, check to make sure puppies have been seen by a veterinarian, and stress that any puppy who is showing signs of illness should stay home. With these precautions in place, starting puppies in my classes when they are eight weeks old has been remarkably successful…for me as an instructor, for the owner, and especially, for the puppy."
–Rebecca S. Lindeman, B.S., Editor of the *Behavior Perspective*

Activity

Bored puppies tend to get in trouble. Many dogs who are given up for adoption were surrendered simply because the owner was not prepared for or could not provide enough stimulation for the breed of dog they acquired. We believe that providing adequate activities and experiences is critical to proper development.

Exercise

Exercise is a key component of the AKC S.T.A.R. Puppy program. The 'A' in S.T.A.R. stands for activity, and activity for puppies means both play and exercise. Sometimes play and exercise overlap so that puppies receive exercise through play activities.

The daily needs for exercise will vary depending on your puppy's age and breed. Within litters, there are also some differences and because some pups may be more or less active than others, their individual exercise needs are different.

Not all play and exercise needs to happen outdoors.

The exercise and play schedules for a puppy are also related to the daily schedule of the owner. AKC S.T.A.R. Puppy Instructor Cheri Yates, PhD, of Best Paw Forward, teaches S.T.A.R. classes at the Seattle Humane Society. To ensure puppies are receiving adequate exercise and play, each owner brings a plan to class called the "Puppy's Exercise, Play and Training Schedule." The schedules have times listed down one side of the page and activities are recorded in boxes. Here are examples in narrative form:

> Mimi, a small mixed breed dog, has an owner that is home during the day. As a result, she has short 5 to 20 minute training or play sessions seven times a day. After breakfast, Mimi is taken for a walk in the neighborhood where walking on a leash and sits are practiced. In late afternoon, she plays ball, and in the evenings, she is taken somewhere for socialization with other dogs and people.

> Chance, a Bernese Mountain Dog, has three very active training and play sessions each day. Each morning, he has a training session to practice S.T.A.R. items followed by a walk lasting at least 20 minutes. At lunchtime, there is another short training session followed by 30 minutes of exercise games in the yard (e.g., "find it!"), and each evening, five minutes of training is followed by grooming activities and a game.

Robin Flaherty and her Poodle mix, Annie, also in the S.T.A.R. class taught by Yates, have a similar schedule involving 3 primary training sessions per day with activities in 10 minute blocks of time. Flaherty uses a clicker to teach skills and she builds in daily socialization and exercise.

As can be seen from the play and exercise schedules designed by these puppy owners, there can be variation in the daily schedule while still meeting the needs of the puppies.

How much exercise?

A general guideline is that puppies can benefit from exercise at least twice a day for about fifteen to thirty minutes. Toy breeds, such as Yorkshire Terriers, can get exercise running up and down a hall in an apartment, whereas exercise for larger breeds most often involves outdoor activity. For some dogs, exercise might mean vigorous play such as chasing a ball, and for others, a walk twice a day can meet the exercise requirements.

There are some considerations when deciding the right amount of exercise for your puppy. For active breeds, putting a dog outside in a fenced yard may not provide enough exercise if the dog does not move around sufficiently on its own. An organized activity that involves your participation may be what is needed to get your dog moving so that she gets health benefits from the exercise.

Some breeds, especially those that are brachycephalic (flat-faced dogs such as Pugs and Bulldogs), are easily overheated and their exercise should be moderated. For puppies, going for a run or jog with you is not an appropriate activity and it can result in injuring your puppy's soft, young joints.

Running on grass and taking a walk with you are good daily exercise choices. For many breeds, as long as the initial instruction is done carefully, swimming provides a great no-impact form of exercise.

S.T.A.R. Story

In the Swim of It

In her AKC S.T.A.R. Puppy classes at Canine Fitness for the Body, Mind and Spirit (Helena, MT), instructor Adele Delp taught puppies (four months or older) to swim. Along with Canine Rehabilitation Practitioner, Jennifer Hill, and with approval from each puppy's veterinarian, Delp taught the lessons in the hydrotherapy pool at the Apex Animal Hospital. To ensure that puppies were safe and not frightened, a systematic shaping program was used. Puppies first got in an empty pool, then in a few inches of water, and when deeper water was introduced, lessons began with puppies in canine life jackets. "The lessons were good for both the puppies and their owners," said Delp. "Puppies learned to swim and their owners learned to teach a skill that involved confidence building. AKC S.T.A.R. Puppy training goes way beyond sit, down and come. These classes teach puppies about the world around them."

The importance of daily exercise

Daily exercise has both mental and physical benefits for your puppy. In addition to providing mental stimulation, there is a saying that "a tired dog is a happy dog," because exercise releases the endorphins that affect the mood and attitude in a positive way.

The physical benefits of exercise for your puppy are many.

- Exercise improves and maintains flexibility along with building strong muscles, joints, and bones.

- Exercise aids digestion. Moving improves motility in the gastro-intestinal tract. This means exercise keeps everything moving so the puppy does not get constipated.

- Exercise strengthens the cardiovascular system (the heart) and helps the respiratory (breathing) system.

- Exercise can help control your puppy's weight and thereby avoid weight-related problems such as diabetes when your dog is older.

- Exercise results in restful sleep, and adequate sleep is necessary to maintain good health.

- When owners are paired with exercise activities (as in your puppy looks forward to you playing ball with her), the bond between the owner and dog is greater.

The effects of exercise on behavior

Exercise can also have a positive effect on reducing any behavior problems that your puppy might have. When dogs have separation issues resulting from being bored, an adequate amount of exercise can actually reduce behaviors such as barking, chewing and destruction. Further, exercise can decrease lethargy and result in a more energetic dog. Exercise can decrease behaviors that make it appear the dog is "hyperactive" when in fact, it is simply in need of more rigorous activity.

S.T.A.R. Story
Not Enough Exercise
Karen Vance is a CGC and AKC S.T.A.R. Puppy instructor. In one of Vance's AKC S.T.A.R. Puppy classes, by the second week, Vance noticed a young German Shepherd Dog who appeared nervous and unable to settle down. As a homework exercise, Vance had the students write down the daily play and exercise routines for their puppies. She started the next class by reviewing these. It turned out the German Shepherd was spending most of his time in the house and he was not receiving regular exercise. "All of a sudden," said Vance, "it all made sense. This puppy, an active herding breed, was not getting the exercise he needed to expend energy. He was about to burst." Vance had a long talk with the owners about the exercise the dog needed. The owners added a daily morning exercise session and an afternoon training session followed by exercise. "Within a week, he was a totally different dog," said Vance. "The owners were happy, I was happy, but most important of all, the dog was happy."

Responsibility

Because we'll talk about the characteristics of a responsible puppy owner in later chapters, we can be brief here. You can guess by now that we believe responsible owners are those that commit to socializing their puppies and providing them with training on basic skills. But that's certainly not all. In addition to teaching their puppies the standard basic behaviors (e.g., sit, down, come), responsible owners teach their puppies what dogs need to know to live in a family. Responsibility means providing an education for a puppy that involves housetraining, crate training and being reliable around other dogs, children and people of all types. Responsible owners clean up after their puppies, they keep their dogs safe with fences and leashes where appropriate, and they provide the necessary routine veterinary care. Finally, responsible owners provide a loving home environment where the needs of puppies and the families they live with are met.

Chapter 2
Before You Get Your Puppy

If you are reading *AKC S.T.A.R. Puppy* because you're thinking about getting a puppy or you want to learn about training the puppy you've been waiting for, we applaud you for doing your homework. A puppy should never be a decision that you make based on emotion. It's easy to fall instantly in love with a little ball of fur that looks like a teddy bear, but this is a long-term commitment and one of the most important relationships you will have in your life. Spend a lot of time doing your research and then ask yourself these questions:

1. Do I have time to give a puppy a quality life?

- Consider if you have time for walks, play and exercise multiple times every single day.

- Can you devote enough time for training?

2. Do I have the financial resources to have a dog? Consider the costs for buying:

- Food.

- Puppy vet visits and any medical emergency treatments.

- Equipment such as leashes and a new fence if needed.

- Training classes.

3. Is my home environment right for a puppy?

- Do you have a fence for a dog who will need exercise?

- Are my children a good match for the puppy I've chosen? A rowdy, 10-year human with behavior problems is not a good match for a fragile puppy.

- Are my other pets a good match for a new puppy? If there is an adult dog in the home with aggression problems you've not yet managed to get under control, this is not the time to add another dog.

- Is the puppy allowed in my condo building or neighborhood?

- If a city resident, are there areas to walk and exercise dogs nearby?

- Is my home or apartment a suitable size for my puppy? As much as you might love them, very active dogs or giant breeds may not do well in a studio apartment in a neighborhood with no grassy areas.

- If the puppy is for the children, is there an adult who is willing to assume all responsibility for the puppy if the children move on to a new interest? (Congratulations, Mom, you got yourself a dog!) *What do puppies and most children have in common?* Answer: *A short attention span.*

4. And the bottom line is, Can I look this puppy in the eyes and say, "I'm here for you for 15 years or as long as you live."

Where to get your puppy

There are a number of places that you can acquire a great puppy. Where you go will depend on a number of factors including whether or not you want a purebred dog from a breeder or a dog from a shelter or rescue group. Considerations for each follow.

This sweet Vizsla puppy will grow up to be an active sporting dog.

Responsible breeders. If you want a purebred puppy, then your first choice should be to find a responsible breeder with expertise in the breed. Responsible breeders breed to improve or maintain a particular breed. They have organized breeding plans and they are well versed in canine genetics. They are involved with their national breed clubs (parent clubs) and they are knowledgeable about any physical or genetic problems in their breed. Dogs who do not meet the written standard for the breed are not bred. Responsible breeders plan litters in advance and most of their puppies have homes waiting before they are born. They also do comprehensive health screening. Contracts with new puppy owners specify that if anything happens to the dog so the owner can not keep it, the dog will be returned to the breeder for placement in a loving home or to live with the breeder. Responsible breeders do not want their dogs to end up in shelters. Many stay in touch with their puppy owners throughout the lifetime of the dog and become like family.

The AKC has a Breeder of Merit Program that is designed to recognize breeders who are committed to both improving their breeds through health testing and selective breeding programs. They also must demonstrate achievements in not only the show ring, but in the field and activities relevant for the breed (http://www.akc.org/breederofmerit/index.cfm).

You can find a list of responsible breeders and Breeder of Merit Participants at www.akc.org.

Rescue organizations. Rescue groups carefully screen dogs and work hard to find them loving homes. There are rescue groups for individual purebred breeds, all-breed rescues and mixed breed rescues. Some rescue groups have a specialty such as hounds, large dogs or Toy breeds. Sometimes dogs in rescue, particularly adult dogs, have behavioral issues. This is not usually the case with puppies, but be sure to ask if the puppy has any behavior problems other than the typical puppy issues such as housetraining and chewing. Rescue volunteers are heroes—many put in long hours and their own money to help the dogs they love. If you have a particular breed you like and you would like to rescue a dog, go to www.akc.org and click on Breeds. On each Breed page, you'll find the link to rescue organizations for that breed.

Shelters. Shelter dogs (whether purebred or mixed breed) can make absolutely wonderful pets and many are having fabulous success in AKC obedience, rally, agility, lure coursing, and most recently, the AKC Therapy Dog program. Be aware, however, that some shelter dogs have behavioral issues. Sometimes the behavioral issues are what got them into the shelter, so be sure to ask about this. If you're an experienced trainer or a beginner who is up for a challenge and willing to get the help you need, rehabilitating a dog who has behavior problems can be extremely rewarding.

Choosing the right dog for you

The very first step in becoming a responsible owner begins the moment you decide to get a dog. Hopefully, you're reading this book before you got your puppy. All dogs are wonderful, but dogs don't come in "one size fits all." Choosing the right dog for you and your family is important in order to live a happy life with your canine family member. The following people and dog characteristics are some things prospective dog owners need to think about.

People characteristics. Look at yourself carefully before getting a puppy. Does your lifestyle lend itself to having a puppy? Are you active or quiet? Do you like being indoors or outdoors? What kind of time can you give to a dog? Do you have any physical/mobility problems?

If you are an athletic, fit runner who wants a pal to run with, as cute as they are, a Basset Hound is not for you. If you are in your senior years, don't care for the outdoors, your favorite activity is sitting in your reclining chair and you just want a furry friend with whom you can enjoy your evening television shows, a herding or sporting dog puppy with a high activity level is not your best choice.

This Greyhound puppy will need plenty of exercise.

How about allergies? If you or someone in your family has allergies, there are some breeds that do better with people who may have allergic reactions to dog dander. We suggest having the allergic person spend time with a prospective dog on several visits to determine if there will be any allergy problems.

Is the time right for you to get a dog? Holidays might seem like the natural time because families have time off from work, but with the hustle, bustle and irregular schedule, this can be a traumatizing time for a new puppy. Choose a time when your life is calm to add a puppy to your family.

Dog characteristics. Do you want a puppy or an adult dog? There is no other joy in the world like a puppy will bring you, but the trade-off is house-training, chewing your shoes and furniture, and the need for training, training, training. Rescuing an older adult dog is one of the most noble things anyone can do. However, you may be in for some veterinary bills if the dog has medical issues or you may find yourself having to un-do bad habits that were reinforced by a previous owner. So be sure to do your homework about any dog you add to your family.

How about size? If you live in a high-rise, small apartment with no outdoor space, a Mastiff may not be the dog for you. If you have young, active, excitable children, a Maltese or Yorkshire Terrier might not be the best breeds for your family. Of course, there are exceptions to every rule. Well-mannered, gentle children who are provided with instruction and adult supervision may do just fine around Toy breeds.

Some puppies, such as this Great Dane, will grow up to be large dogs.

Coat type. If you live with someone who hates wearing clothes that are covered with dog hair and you don't especially like to vacuum, even though you love those blue eyes, a Siberian Husky or other furry dog with an undercoat that sheds is not the breed for you. You would do better to choose a flat-coated or less shedding breed. Some dog lovers will choose a dog with coat type being a major consideration. Loving a furry soft coat and curly spaniel ears, some prospective owners would rather not have a flat-coated breed. There are breeds that look their best when they are well groomed. If you're not prepared to learn how to groom a dog, then you need to consider if you can afford regular hair appointments for both you and your dog.

Temperament. There are some breeds that are generally more active (think of what they were bred to do…as in, Border Collies can run ALL DAY herding sheep) and some breeds that are quiet. Know also that within an individual litter, there are puppies who are more active, and puppies who are quiet and more submissive. A responsible breeder who knows dogs will help you select the puppy that is the right match for you.

No matter what breed you choose, all dogs deserve training and the AKC S.T.A.R. Puppy and Canine Good Citizen Program are great ways to accomplish it.

Advice from experts for the new puppy owner

The following people are regarded as international experts when it comes to their breeds and dogs in general. Each one has

Some breeds of puppies will require a lot of grooming as adults.

had personal experience with hundreds of dogs. We've categorized breeds into the AKC groups and added a special category for mixed breed dogs whose heritage is not always known. To learn more about a specific breed or Group, visit www.akc.org and click on Breeds.

Herding (Michele Ritter, Britannia Beardies)

Known as a breeder, owner and handler of some of the finest Bearded Collies in the country, Michele Ritter's puppies are also known for their performance abilities in obedience, agility, rally, herding, and just about every other dog sport. When Ritter talks about what herding breed puppies need, she sounds like she is reading directly from the AKC S.T.A.R. Puppy playbook. "Because herding breeds are sensitive, as puppies they need a lot of exposure to different stimuli. Exposing them to city traffic, going where they can meet new people such as at a soccer match, and taking them to a community event are just some examples of the varied experiences these dogs need as puppies.

Especially for the long-haired breeds like the Beardie, you've got to start exposing the puppy early to the grooming table, grooming tools, and the noise and feel of the air from a dryer."

"New puppy owners need to understand that herding breeds were bred to chase," says Ritter. "As far as a herding breed is concerned, if it moves, it can be chased. That includes children, bicycles, and cars. Training is very important so the chasing can be controlled when necessary and channeled into an appropriate activity such as chasing a ball, or better yet, herding."

Ritter encourages puppy owners to take their puppies to training classes. Herding dogs are quick learners and in class, the owner can learn how to train these fast, intelligent canines. Because they have such a work ethic, some of the breed standards for herding breeds say they are aloof with strangers. "For some," explains Ritter, "it just appears they aren't interested in strangers. Trust me, they've got their eye on the person. My dog, Spot, played hard to get. Then he would come up and sit beside a person. He would start nuzzling them, until he was gently nibbling at the nape of their neck. He had this routine worked out to a science—he would work around to the person's ear and before she knew what was happening, Spot would remove her earrings."

Hounds (Michael Canalizo, AKC Director of Event Planning)
Michael Canalizo has owned, trained, bred, judged and loved hounds for the better part of his life. The Afghan Hounds he has trained and shown have been the top-winning hounds of all times. Completely dispelling the myth that hounds aren't smart, Canalizo was a nationally recognized handler who got every hound he worked with to do exactly what he wanted it to do. "Don't let the hound breeds fool you," says Canalizo. "They are incredibly smart. They don't suffer fools gladly and if you want them to do tasks like obedience training, you have to make the dog think the training was his idea."

When asked what advice he would give to a first time puppy buyer of an Afghan or another hound breed, Canalizo didn't pause for a second. "First," he said, "you've got to realize that with hounds, instinct lays just below the surface at all times. This means even though your puppy is looking serene, regal, and calm, you can't trust an untrained dog to be off leash. At the first sign of something to chase, a sighthound will be off and running and there's not a human on this planet fast enough to catch one."

Canalizo pointed out how hounds, who aren't often given enough credit for being clever, are problem solvers. "You not only need to be extremely vigilant about keeping the gates closed, but for breeds like Afghans, putting locks on the gates is sometimes necessary. I've had Afghans who could open the refrigerator. With some of them, it was like living with a bad college roommate. With one dog, I once opened the refrigerator only to discover that the turkey I planned on having for lunch was gone. I remember another time when "Buzzy," a top winning Afghan, opened the refrigerator and helped himself to some lemon pie. He could pull the refrigerator door open and then it would swing closed on its own. When I came in the room, Buzzy tried his best to maintain an innocent look, but I knew the second I saw the meringue on his chin, it was time to put a lock on the refrigerator."

Non Sporting (Cody Sickle, Cherokee Bulldogs)

The AKC Non-Sporting group consists of breeds that are extremely varied in size, shape and temperament. A popular Non-Sporting breed is the Bulldog. Cody Sickle has been involved with Bulldogs for more than 50 years. He's an AKC judge and he's judged Bulldogs internationally. Sickle's love of the breed started when he was 5 years old. He saw Bulldogs on cartoons and asked for one. Finally, when he was eight years old, he got his dog. Sickle was one of the children we talk about who are the "exception to the rule," in that he was kind, gentle, responsible, and wanted to spend time with his dog. His was not a situation where the child got a dog and within a few months, his mother had a Bulldog.

Surprisingly, for someone who is at the top of the game in the conformation dog show world, Sickle advises first time Bulldog owners to do what he did with his first dog—join an obedience club and start training. "The benefit of training classes and joining a club," says Sickle, "is you can find a mentor to help you and inspire you. In my case, there were two brothers who were older than me. They were doing a great job with their Sheltie and I wanted to be a good trainer like them. I could eventually work my dog off lead and I had good control. She lagged a little and did not hurry, but she was reliable enough for me to be successful at obedience."

Sickle advises new puppy owners to take their puppies to a training class. "With Bulldogs, and many other breeds," he says, "classes teach you, as the owner, how to teach your puppy to be a terrific member of your family. I tell everyone to involve the whole family in the dog's training." Sickle shows his dogs under the name of that very first Bulldog, "Cherokee." "I was just a kid and I thought dogs had the middle initial and last name of the owner," Sickle explained, "so, I named her, 'Cherokee T. Sickle.' That was her registered name." A dignified and respectable name for a dog who taught her owner so much.

Sporting (Doug Johnson, Clussexx Clumber Spaniels)
Known for his Clumber and Sussex Spaniels, AKC judge and 2009 Breeder of the Year Doug Johnson knows and understands sporting dogs, especially spaniels. "The spaniels make great family dogs," Johnson says. "They've got a natural willingness to please, they're outgoing, they love people, and they're very sociable."

But he's quick to add, "That said, spaniels are sensitive creatures. They can be reserved with people they don't know and if they haven't received a lot of socialization, they look at the outside world with caution."

For that reason, Johnson stresses the importance of early socialization. "We tell people that they are adding a new member to their family and they need to be ready for the challenge of raising a sporting dog. Puppies need training, and I like to maintain a relationship with puppy owners as their dogs grow up. This includes family pets (who all must be spayed or neutered) who won't be shown in conformation. "I believe that correct puppy socialization is one of the most important parts of raising dogs," said Johnson.

Even if your sporting breed puppy is primarily a pet, there will be times when you will see your dog's hunting heritage come shining through. Johnson recalls a story of a Clumber Spaniel he owned in college.

"This particular dog was one of my early conformation dogs. He was gorgeous and he won the National Specialty twice. A good friend of mine had a pond on her property. When a fox killed one of her beautiful Canadian Geese, my friend was so distraught that she took the goose to a taxidermist. The goose held a place of honor on the top of a 6 ft. bookshelf. I went to visit with my dog and my friend and I went out for dinner. When we returned, there was stuffing everywhere, what remained of the goose was scattered around the den, and with his head held high, my Clumber proudly carried a wing around the room. He may have been a top winning conformation dog, but he was first and foremost, a sporting dog."

Johnson offers first time puppy owners four extremely valuable tips:

1. Learn everything you can about dogs, your breed and then about your individual dog.

2. Network to meet people who can help you learn about dogs and support you as you train your puppy. AKC dog clubs are a great way to network.

3. Find a mentor. This can be your breeder or a great instructor in a puppy training class.

4. Set goals for you and your puppy. For some people, the goal will be winning one of this country's biggest dog shows. For others, it will be to have your sporting breed puppy go on to become a therapy dog or work in the field. And for many other people, the goal may be simply having a well-behaved pet who knows how to come when called and follow basic commands.

"The advice for sporting dogs really pertains to all dogs," says Johnson. "They need an adequate amount of exercise, early socialization that is ongoing throughout the dog's life, and training to teach them to be good citizens."

Terrier (Barbara Miller, Max-Well Norfolk Terriers)

For Barbara Miller, 2007 AKC Breeder of the Year, placing a puppy is serious business. Because she loves her puppies and wants to ensure they'll have great homes, a prospective owner must start with a telephone session with Miller that lasts at least 25 minutes. Answering questions via email isn't an option because Miller wants to hear the inflections in a person's voice and take note of spontaneous comments. The phone interview is just the beginning of the education process for a new puppy owner that will last throughout the dog's life.

Miller provides prospective puppy owners practical information and she quickly dispenses of rumors such as "females are sweeter." She emphasizes the importance of a well-constructed fence for terrier puppies. "Norfolks and a number of the other terriers go to ground, so a buried fence is essential even if the dog is only left for five minutes unsupervised," advises Miller.

When prospective puppy owners have a child, Miller wants to meet both the child and parents. "It is very important for the mom in the house to want the dog because there's a good chance she's going to end up taking the puppy to the vet, shopping for food and supplies, caring for the coat and cleaning up after the puppy," says Miller. "When I grew up, I was the rare child who was ready, willing and able to care for a dog. Children who get a puppy and don't lose interest in it are unique, and this is why I make sure there is at least one adult in every family who is committed to having a dog. When you do find that unique child, being a mentor is such a joy."

Coat care for Norfolk Terriers is important; brushing and combing is advised at least three times per week for pet dogs. While crate training is an important tool for housetraining, Miller advises that crates should not be over-used and a puppy should never be crated all day.

Miller suggests starting training for terriers when they are puppies. "Norfolks are affectionate, wonderful dogs who are as at home in a city apartment as they are in the suburbs. To fully enjoy a terrier breed, you should provide them with training that is fair and consistent. Once they figure out that you're the boss, they do very well in obedience, agility, and go-to-ground activities."

Toy (Carol Harris, Bo-Bett Italian Greyhounds)

"When many people think of Toy breeds, they think of shaky, little nervous dogs," explained Carol Harris, of Bo-Bett Italian Greyhounds. "These breeds shouldn't be like that—when the breeding is left to knowledgeable, responsible breeders who only breed dogs with good temperaments, we see confident, steady, happy dogs."

Harris describes Italian Greyhounds as "tiny elegant sight hounds that are loads of fun to play with, train, show, and love." Italian Greyhounds, also known as IGs, are extremely intelligent, athletic, and "faster than lightning," says Harris. "They may appear like small Greyhounds but it is important to know that the temperament of Toy breeds can be different than those that appear to be simply a larger version of the dog. For example, IGs are more sensitive and fragile minded than Whippets or Greyhounds and you need to take this into account when training an IG."

As a breeder of top-winning Whippets and Italian Greyhounds, Harris offers great advice for first time owners of Toy breeds. It pertains to any breed actually. "Work hard to familiarize yourself with the breed," she says. "You should not only learn about the breed in general but the breeders and specific dogs within the breed." Italian Greyhounds are loving dogs and they try very hard to please their owners. As with many Toy breeds, they have little tolerance for loud, insensitive people. For this reason, when Harris only places a puppy in a family with children after meeting the children and determining they are sensible and obedient.

"How you raise a Toy breed makes all the difference," says Harris. "They may be Toy breeds but they aren't *toy dogs* that need to be carried around. Starting early with letting them be dogs who run and jump and play teaches them to use their bodies and this will prevent accidents later." Harris stresses the importance of ongoing, continued socialization for Toy breeds. "Their health and personality depends a great deal on the amount of time we spend with them," she says. Throughout the day, Harris advises puppy owners to use daily routines such as feeding to teach the puppy good manners. For example, Harris requires all of her dogs to wait politely before receiving a treat.

Good manners, socialization, careful placement of dogs with families, and leaving the breeding to responsible, knowledgeable breeders… the advice Carol Harris gives us for the Toy breeds pertains to all dogs.

Working (Jean Boyd, Rivergroves Great Pyrenees)
Jean Boyd has more than 40 years experience with Great Pyrenees and many people know about her Best in Show dogs. A less known fact is that Boyd's early experience in the breed included a High-in-Trial obedience dog, and her dogs have been successful at agility, obedience, and therapy work. "They're versatile and multi-talented," says Boyd. "This breed, like many working breeds, is also great at backpacking, walking, jogging and at the other end of the continuum, after receiving adequate exercise, they make fabulous couch potatoes."

The Great Pyrenees is a livestock guard dog. "Working dogs that have been bred to do a job on their own will tire of repetitive training. It is very important to use positive training methods and make the training interesting and fun," Boyd advises. "When you think of working breeds, remember that these dogs were bred to work in close contact with a person. This means that they don't tolerate being alone for extended periods of time. Even though many of the breeds may be large and have a lot of hair, they need to spend time in the house with their human families."

As advised in the Canine Good Citizen Responsible Dog Owner's Pledge, Boyd agrees there should be parental supervision whenever the Great Pyrenees and young children are together. Asked if there were any specific recommendations for first time owners of a working breed, Boyd said, "Fences are important so your puppy can stay safe while getting enough exercise. We advise all owners of new puppies to take their dogs to puppy classes. In addition to the ability to learn basic behaviors such as sit, down and so on, puppies really benefit from the socialization with people and other dogs in classes. Look for an instructor who knows how to teach while keeping it fun."

One parent described the impact that one of Boyd's dogs had in her family's life:

> "We were ready for a dog and after much research, went to visit Jean and her dogs. Our youngest son, John, has dyspraxia, a disorder that affects speech and language. Our children played with the dogs as we talked to Jean. As we were leaving, we heard someone say, 'Bye bye, dog!' Everyone stopped, stared, and with our mouths wide open, we all said, 'Did you hear that?!' Motivated by a Great Pyrenees, John had spoken his very first sentence."

Mixed breed dogs

Known also as All-American dogs, mixed breed dogs, as well as purebreds, make wonderful pets when they are properly screened, matched to the right person or family and provided with training. There are mixed breed dogs in all shapes and sizes. If the parentage of mixes is unknown, people tend to think of them as "types," such as a "terrier type," "hound mix" or "lab type" dog. Sometimes, shelter staff will take their best guess based on the appearance of the dog and write, "Lab x Chow" on the kennel card to indicate these are the two breeds likely to be the dog's parents. However, when you have a mixed breed dog in a shelter, remember there is often a good chance that dog had two mixed breed parents who each had mixed breed parents, and what you actually may have standing before you is a combination of eight or more breeds. Several DNA tests for identifying breeds are on the market for those dog owners who want to know about their puppy's ancestry. Not all breeds are identified yet, but until they are, you can make your best guess and provide training based on sound scientific principles.

Chapter 3

Your Puppy Comes Home

So you've finally taken that big step and added a puppy to your household. For many people, this is one of the greatest times of their lives. There's really nothing like waking up in the morning and seeing the sweet face of a puppy who completely trusts and adores you. But, as joyful as it is, there are some practical issues and challenges that you'll need to address when raising your puppy.

One of the main challenges is dealing with housetraining. If there is anything that makes people give up on a dog and take it to the shelter in a hurry, it is when the dog is not housetrained and continues to soil in the house. Ruined carpets and urine stained hardwood that will cost a lot of money to clean or repair are just a little too much for some owners to bear. The consequences when a dog is not housetrained can be very serious, ranging from the dog being unfairly punished, to being sentenced to a life in the backyard, to being taken to a shelter for a problem that could be solved if the owner had the proper help.

This section will give you some tips on how to housetrain your puppy and how you can use a crate to help with that process as well as prevent your puppy from destroying your home.

We've already talked about teething and how the key to managing chewing is managing the environment. Using a crate effectively will also help you manage your puppy's environment.

Housetraining your puppy

Puppies are most effectively housetrained using a combination of crate training and taking them outside for a walk on leash to a designated spot on a regular schedule. (Small dogs who live in apartments in urban areas can be paper trained). The details of using a crate as part of a housetraining program are discussed later in this chapter.

If you are going to housetrain your puppy to go outside, AKC S.T.A.R. Puppy Item #14 Walks on a leash will be a very important and useful skill when it comes to housetraining your dog. You'll want to take your puppy to an acceptable outdoor area for urinating and defecating and having a dog that is under control when walking on a leash makes getting there easier.

Tips for housetraining

1. **Understand your puppy.** Puppies don't urinate or defecate inside to annoy you. Housetraining is a learning process. Young puppies do not yet have the bladder and bowel control to 'hold it' for long periods of time.

   Trainers often use the month of age rule to determine how long a puppy should be expected to go between trips outside. A puppy younger than four weeks of age needs to be in the whelping box and a place where he has access to papers or puppy pads. At one month old, it is reasonable to expect a puppy to go about an hour before urinating again. Using the month rule, at two months old the puppy can go two hours, three month old puppies can go three hours, and so on.

   For maximum housetraining success, we suggest taking your young puppy outside at least every two hours. In addition to going outside for playtime, don't forget to take your puppy outside when he wakes up, after meals and right before bed. If your puppy is having accidents in the house, try taking him outside more frequently.

   If you have a long workday and need to leave your puppy at home, consider a dog walker or puppy day care. Provide your puppy with a safe space that is an adequate size if the puppy will be alone more than a few hours. The space should have a place to nap, water, treats, toys, plenty of room to walk around and papers or puppy pads for housetraining.

2. **Establish a consistent feeding schedule** and based on that, establish your housetraining schedule for trips outside.

3. **Walk your puppy *on leash* to the area that you've designated as the bathroom.**

4. **Just as your puppy starts to relieve himself, say whatever words you will use from now on to signal to the puppy that this is a good place to go.** You can say, "Go potty," "Go here" or whatever term you choose, but keep it consistent. As soon as the puppy is finished, praise him by saying something like, "Good boy, go potty!" In the beginning, you'll should give the verbal cue exactly when the puppy is relieving himself. He'll soon make the connection between your verbal cue and what you want him to do.

5. **Understand the importance of moving.** Moving around, either by walking or playtime, will stimulate your puppy's bladder and bowels. Give your puppy enough time and exercise when you are on a housetraining walk.

6. **Accidents happen.** If your puppy has an accident, do not punish her. When you catch her in the act, if she is a small puppy, you can pick her up and go out the door. If she is a larger dog and if she knows "come," you can call her to come to you so you can take her outside. Otherwise, go and get her and take her outside. Walk her on leash to the outdoor bathroom area. Clean up the accident with an enzyme cleaner that removes the odor.

Crate training for safety, separation issues and housetraining

Crate training is used for two primary purposes: 1) to keep your puppy safe while you are away from home; and 2) to assist with housetraining. If the puppy is crated, she can't pull down the Christmas tree, escape like a convict from a screened window or chew your computer's electrical wires. While you're gone, you'll have the peace of mind that comes from knowing your puppy won't get an intestinal obstruction from eating a large portion of a stuffed chair and a box of pencils.

The other major use of crate training, as a tool to housetrain your puppy, is based on the idea that puppies don't want to soil their immediate area and by using a crate, you can teach them to wait until they are taken outside to relieve themselves. Whatever the reason you are teaching your puppy to feel comfortable in a crate, the training principles are the same. Your puppy will learn that his crate is a place where he can go to rest and feel secure. Many dogs get to the point that if the crate door is left open, they will go in and out of the crate on their own.

S.T.A.R. Story

My parents were dog lovers, and when I grew up, we always had dogs. This was back before pet dog owners knew about crate training so our dogs never had crates. As an adult, I invited my parents to come to a dog show to watch me compete in obedience. When I came out of the ring with my Border Collie, I said "Let's put him in his crate and look around the dog show." My parents were horrified; they had seen crates everywhere at the show, but they never dreamed my dog would be crated. I opened the door of Laddie's crate and he nearly knocked them down getting inside. When we came back from walking around, Laddie was sleeping on his back with his feet up in the air and he was snoring. My parents witnessed firsthand how a dog views and welcomes his crate as a quiet respite.

Choosing a crate

There are several types of crates from which you can choose. You can find crates in pet stores, catalogs or from online pet supply sources.

- **Plastic crates** that are plastic with vents on each side and a wire door in front are often referred to as "airline crates" because this is the only style of crate allowed by airlines. If you choose a plastic crate, make sure the crate is placed in a well-ventilated area since a large part of the crate is solid.

- **Wire crates** come in a variety of styles including solid wire crates and those that collapse and fold like a suitcase. If you are using a crate as your puppy's den and a place to sleep, you can cover the top with a towel to block out the light. Even a puppy needs privacy!

- **Fabric crates** are usually made of tough nylon. Somewhat like tents for dogs, they are collapsible and have a zipper opening. Anyone who has carried a heavy metal crate or large airline crate from a parking lot into a building will tell you that these featherweight crates are fabulous. And they are—for when the dog is trained or you are there to supervise. With a young untrained puppy, particularly one with separation issues, you might come home to find your puppy has chewed her way out of her crate.

What size crate should I buy?

Whatever type of crate you select for your puppy, it should be big enough that the puppy can stand up, lie down and stretch out, and turn around.

Crates for housetraining

If you are buying a crate for the purposes of housetraining, many trainers will recommend that the crate not be too big. For example, if the primary goal is housetraining your Yorkshire Terrier, buying a crate for a Great Dane just so your puppy has more room will defeat the purpose when it comes to housetraining. Crate training works because dogs don't like to soil the area in which they sleep. If you buy a huge crate for a tiny dog, there is a good chance there will be enough space for your puppy to designate a 'bathroom' area within the crate.

How long should puppies be in a crate?

If you are primarily using your puppy's crate to keep her safe while you are gone and she is already housetrained, you may decide to choose a crate that is larger to give your dog more freedom of movement.

If your puppy is under six months old, he should never be left in the crate for more than three to four hours at a time and younger puppies should go out at least every two hours. Younger puppies have less bowel and bladder control and can't be expected to go several hours without relieving themselves.

But, the reality is you have a job that you need to be at for eight hours and travel each way takes forty minutes. Now what? Consider a puppy walker to come in mid-day or puppy day care. If that doesn't work for you, another option is to use plastic fencing or baby gates to mark off an area such as a kitchen or large bathroom. Put the crate in the corner so your puppy can take a nap. Leave your puppy with a treat, fresh water and interactive toys. Papers or puppy pads in the corner will be the place for the puppy to relieve himself. This might make the outdoor housetraining process take a little longer, but your puppy's welfare comes first.

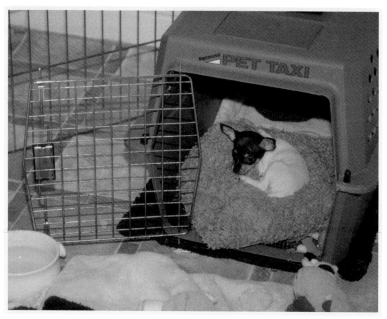

If you have to be gone extended periods of time, make sure your puppy is comfortable by not restricting him to the crate.

Crate training your puppy: A positive step by step approach

1. **Getting comfortable with the crate.** Leave the door of the crate open and put the crate in a place where you and the puppy spend time together. Put comfortable bedding in the crate, such as a crate pad, or a towel with your scent on it.

2. **Get your puppy used to being around and inside the crate.** Put some of your puppy's treats near the opening of the crate. Then, put some just inside the crate. The puppy will probably stay on the outside, lean in, and take the treat. Next, throw a treat inside the crate. When the puppy is inside getting the treat, praise her, "Good girl in your crate!" Start teaching a verbal cue to signal your puppy to go in the crate. For example, just as she is starting to go into the crate to get the treat, say, "Go crate," "Kennel up," or whatever your cue will be.

3. **Feed dinner in the crate.** After your puppy is going into the crate to get a treat, feed her in the crate. Put her food bowl in the crate but leave the door open.

4. **Feed dinner in the crate with the door closed.** The next step is to close the door of the crate while your puppy is eating.

5. **Use shaping while training.** Gradually lengthen the time your puppy is in the crate after eating before you open the door.

6. **Practice short times in the crate when you don't need to leave.** Instruct your dog to go in the crate, when she goes in, give her a treat, then close the door. Build up the length of time your puppy will stay in the crate. Leave the immediate area of the crate, go somewhere else in the room where your puppy can see you. Gradually increase the time your puppy is in the crate.

7. **Practice leaving your puppy in the crate, leaving the room, and returning.** Start with leaving a short time, then gradually add time.

8. **Drum roll...**now it's time for the big step, leaving the house for a short time. With your puppy in her crate, leave the house for a few minutes. Give your puppy a consistent cue each time you leave such as saying, "Watch the house," or "I'll be back." Your puppy will learn that this is a routine and each and every time, you come back.

9. **See you later.** When you leave your puppy, leave with a cheerful, confident tone in your voice. Don't hug, pet, and talk to the puppy like you will never see her again. If you do this, your puppy will pick up on your emotions and will get stressed when you leave.

10. **"I'm home."** When you return home after being gone, calmly open the crate door and say hello to the puppy. Let the puppy outside or go for a walk so the puppy can relieve herself.

When crate training is done properly, your dog will go in the crate on her own.

Following these steps will help you train your puppy so that she will eventually go in the crate on her own. AKC S.T.A.R. Puppy Item #20, Stays on leash with another person (while the owner walks away and returns), teaches your puppy that there are times when you need to leave but you will come back. In the puppy classes, your instructor can help you learn practical skills related to you and your puppy being separated such as crate training and dealing with separation behaviors.

Chapter 4

AKC S.T.A.R Puppy Test: Owner Behaviors

The following six skills from the AKC S.T.A.R. Puppy test relate primarily to the other end of the leash, the owner. In this chapter, we'll provide you with information on learning each of these S.T.A.R. skills:

1. **Maintains puppy's health (vaccines, exams, appears healthy)**

2. **Owner receives Responsible Dog Owner's Pledge**

3. **Owner describes adequate daily play and exercise plan**

4. **Owner and puppy attend at least six classes by an AKC Approved CGC Evaluator**

5. **Owner brings bags to classes for cleaning up after puppy**

6. **Owner has obtained some form of ID for puppy (collar tag, microchip)**

S.T.A.R. Item #1.
**Maintains the puppy's health
(vaccines, exams, appears healthy)**

In AKC S.T.A.R. classes, your instructor will ask you to present proof that your puppy is in the care of a veterinarian (e.g., record of initial exam, vaccines). In the beginning of each class, instructors take a few minutes to present a "Lesson for the Puppy's People." It is during this time that your instructor can review and talk to you about your puppy's diet and feeding schedule. As a homework exercise, you may be asked to bring a written copy of your puppy's daily activity and exercise plan. By finding out in class what you're doing with regard to your puppy's diet, exercise, training and activities, your instructor can give you feedback and helpful hints for new activities.

Finding the right veterinarian for your puppy

As a new puppy owner, your veterinarian will be the first professional that you will come to know and trust. Maintaining the physical health of your precious puppy provides the critical foundation that is needed so your dog can learn, develop good social relationships and enjoy a lifetime of activities and fun with you.

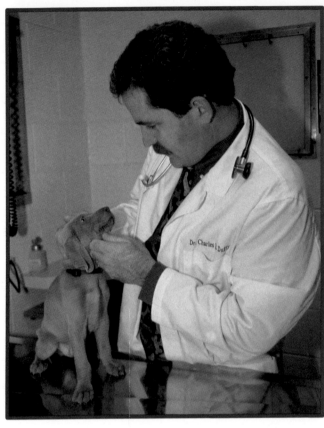

The veterinarian is the first professional a new puppy owner will come to know and trust.

As soon as you decide to add a new puppy to your family, find the veterinarian that is the best match for you and your dog. Of course, if you have other pets, you may already have a vet and you're all set. But, if you need to begin the search to find a health care provider for your pup, here are some tips:

1. Get recommendations from people you trust. You might know someone who is involved in dogs either as a breeder, long time exhibitor, instructor or trainer. A recommendation from someone who is dog knowledgeable will provide a head start in finding the veterinarian who best meets the needs of your puppy.

2. Set up an interview (with the veterinarian and staff). There is a tendency for dog owners to choose a veterinarian by looking on the internet and selecting the animal hospital closest to them. If you don't know someone who could give you a recommendation and you're starting cold, you can certainly begin with a veterinarian who is close to home. However, keep in mind that if there is a medical crisis with your puppy, you want to be in the hands of a vet who is up to

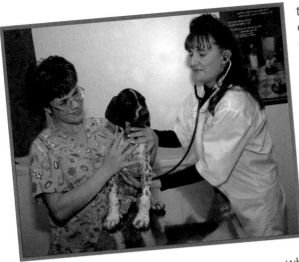

the task. Driving another five miles in exchange for peace of mind will be well worth the extra time and trouble.

Call the office and make an appointment to talk to the vet and take a tour. If you are told the clinic does not give tours or appointments to meet the staff, this is not where you want to be for your dog's healthcare. Some veterinary clinics have web pages that will answer many of your questions, but reading a web page is not a good substitute for meeting the veterinarian in person.

3. Arrange a meet and greet interview with the vet and staff. Before going to meet the veterinarian and staff, develop a list of questions and take the written questions with you. This will keep you on track, and will help you be more organized. Introduce yourself and briefly tell the veterinarian about your puppy. Be respectful of the staff and veterinarian's time and keep this meeting brief. Sample questions for your personalized checklist include:

- Pay attention to basic credentials. Are AVMA and AAHA certificates displayed on the wall? AVMA, the American Veterinary Medical Association, is the accreditation body for veterinarians. AAHA, the American Animal Hospital Association, shows that the animal hospital has met standards of quality care.

- Veterinarian's credentials, credentials of other staff (e.g., do you have veterinary technicians)? If my puppy has a specific problem such as she requires a surgery or eye problem, do you have a specialty in the area or will we be referred to a specialist?

- What is your position on vaccines? How often do you vaccinate? What do you vaccinate for? It is most common for puppies to receive vaccinations at six weeks of age, then a booster every three weeks until the puppy is sixteen weeks old.

- What regular care will my puppy receive? We suggest for a healthy puppy an annual physical, fecal, heartworm check in addition to initial vaccines and boosters. Ask about surgeries your puppy may need such as being spayed or neutered.

- What do you suggest for my puppy's diet?

- What do you recommend for spay/neuter? At what age should my puppy be spayed/neutered?

- Emergency care. If my puppy has a medical emergency, does the clinic provide emergency service or is there a phone number for a local emergency clinic?

- Training and Special Services. Do you have obedience training at the clinic? Do you recommend or work with a trainer/animal behaviorist? What methods does your trainer use and what is her philosophy? Do you make house calls? Who is your back-up when you are gone? Since you have more than one vet, can I see the vet of my choice? Is there grooming at the clinic? Who does the grooming, when, and what is the fee?

- Do you have boarding at the clinic? Is the clinic staffed around the clock on evenings and weekends?

- Have you ever worked with my breed before? If the answer is "no," this is your chance to give a 30-second education about any breed characteristics that the vet should know about. "My breed can have problems with anesthesia. Have you worked with this breed before?" Or, "My dog is a shelter dog; have you worked with many shelter dogs who have issues similar to those my dog has?"

- Hours and fees. When is the clinic open? If you have a work schedule that restricts when you can take your puppy to veterinary appointments, move this question to the top of the list and ask it during the initial phone contact. If the only time you can take your dog to the veterinarian is Saturday morning, and the clinic is only open 8 am to 5 pm Monday through Friday, you don't need to waste your time (or more importantly, the veterinarian's time) asking all of the above questions.

- Ideally, your puppy will have a great life free of illness. But, in life, things happen and for that reason, be sure to ask, "In case of an emergency, will my puppy be seen if I bring her here? If my dog is sick and requires overnight care, is someone here with him?"

- Do you participate with a pet insurance plan?"
- Finally, inquire about the fees for specific services, but remember that your puppy's health should be in the hands of a veterinarian you trust. Searching for veterinary care based on the lowest cost or a convenient location is not the approach to take when it comes to the puppy you love.

4. Tour the clinic from the front lobby to the back kennel. This will tell you a lot about the quality of care in this animal hospital. The facility should be clean and free from offensive odors. If the lobby is full of stressed-out pets and pet owners who appear to have been waiting for an hour, remember, this could be you. Are the staff working at the front desk courteous, knowledgeable and helpful? Is there a separate area for dogs and cats, or are appointments scheduled so that the lobby does not become crowded? Are exam rooms clean and sterilized after each pet? Is the kennel area clean and pleasant? If you are boarding your dog, take note of the size of the kennels and the temperature. Is the kennel air-conditioned and heated?

5. Attend the first visit with your puppy. Many dog owners know in an instant whether they feel a veterinarian is a good match. The responses you get to questions during the interview as well as how the veterinarian interacts with your puppy will help you make a decision.

S.T.A.R. Story

"I had a lot of friends who were dog trainers and my veterinarian came highly recommended," said Scott. "On the first visit, Dr. Purvis walked into the room. He was polite and friendly and introduced himself. And within seconds, he was on his knees on the floor talking to and petting my dog. He didn't have eye contact with me for the next several minutes. It was all about the dog. My dog was in heaven, wagging his tail and acting as though the veterinarian was his long lost friend. I was sold. He had my dog at hello, there was no question that this was the vet for us."

6. Say "Aaaah:" The Physical Exam. To avoid diseases that other canine patients may have had, when you attend the first few visits, if possible, carry your puppy into the clinic. On the first visit with your puppy, observe how the veterinarian and staff handle and interact with your dog. If an assistant is abrupt when handling the dog in an exam room when you are present, this is not a good sign for what might happen when you're not there.

During the physical exam, the veterinarian will check your dog from head to toe. The eyes and nose will be examined to make sure there is no discharge or infection. The veterinarian will look into the puppy's ears to check for odors indicating infection or parasites such as mites. The mouth, teeth and gums will be checked for any unusual growths, color or dental problems. The skin will be checked for any unusual growths or problems such as dermatitis or parasites such as fleas or ticks. The veterinarian will also check your puppy's feet.

In addition to looking at the outside of the dog, a stethoscope will be used to check your puppy's heart, lungs and bowel sounds. The vet will feel the puppy's belly to rule out obvious problems. For female pups, the genitals will be checked to ensure there is no discharge or infection. For males, the veterinarian will check to see if the testicles are descended. Undescended testicles can be related to hormone or endocrine problems.

10 signs your puppy needs a trip to the veterinarian

1. Diarrhea, vomiting or constipation (or in general, changes in bladder/bowel habits or set-back in housetraining).

2. Fever. Puppy temperature should be 100 to 102.5 degrees. The temperature of newborn puppies is lower (about 94 degrees) and it gradually increases over time. Watch for shivering or panting or any indication of tremors or seizures.

3. Refusing food or water.

4. Signs of pain (whines, cries, bites/snaps if touched, can't move, limps, won't get up).

5. Breathing problems (such as wheezing, panting, gagging, coughing).

6. Discharge from the eyes or nose.

7. Urine/bladder problems (straining to urinate, bloody urine, or excessive urination).

8. Injuries (swelling, cuts, bleeding, puncture wounds).

9. Activity level changes (very hyperactive behavior, lethargic behavior, change in sleep pattern) or changes in how the puppy moves (unsteady gait).

10. Symptoms related to the mouth or ears (blood from ears, shaking head, pale gums, drooling).

As the exam progresses, when the veterinarian gets to the "other end" of the puppy, a stool sample will be collected and your puppy's temperature will be taken. It should be between 100 and 102.5 degrees Fahrenheit.

The stool sample and a blood test will reveal whether or not the puppy has roundworms, heartworms, hookworms, or tapeworms and a course of treatment will be prescribed if parasites are present.

Vaccines

If the puppy is vaccinated on the first visit, does the staff take time to remind you about the purpose of the vaccines? When you check out, are you given written instructions for signs and symptoms to monitor following vaccines or medical treatments?

Vaccines for dogs are divided into two categories: 1) core vaccines, which are those that all dogs must have; and 2) non-core vaccines, which are those that are recommended in certain situations where there is a risk of exposure (such as if a dog is boarded with many other dogs, or if a dog is frequently exposed to ticks or creeks that may be infected). Core vaccines include those for distemper, canine hepatitis, parvovirus, and rabies. Non-core vaccines are parainfluenza, Bordatella (kennel cough), coronavirus, leptospirosis, and Lyme.

At early visits with the veterinarian, your puppy will also be dewormed.

While there may be variations in vaccines depending on the laws of your state with regard to certain vaccines and the schedule the veterinarian determines is best for your puppy, a typical vaccination plan is:

5 weeks: Parvovirus

6 to 8 weeks: Combination vaccine for:

- Canine Hepatitis (adenovirus)
- Distemper

- Parainfluenza
- Parvovirus

12 weeks: Rabies

12 to 15 weeks: In locations where there may be a problem:

- Leptospirosis
- Coronavirus
- Lyme Disease (typically two boosters)

14 to 16 weeks: Combination vaccine (Boosters) that is called DHLPP for:

- Distemper
- Hepatitis
- Leptospirosis
- Parainfluenza
- Parvovirus.

Holistic veterinary care

As an alternative to a traditional vaccine schedule, holistic or natural veterinarians rely upon a blood test called "titer testing" to determine which vaccines are necessary for your pet. You can learn more about holistic veterinary care online or from a holistic veterinarian in your area.

Your puppy's diet: What's for dinner?

Before we talk about food, puppies should always have access to clean water. Water is essential for maintaining health, keeping your pup's organs healthy and for preventing dehydration. Dog bowls and dishes should be cleaned every day and made of material that does not harbor germs.

Types of food

There are three categories of dog foods including kibble (hard pieces), canned food and semi-moist food. Some loving owners think that there is only one category of food for their beloved puppy and it is called people food. While the occasional people food treat won't hurt your puppy, dogs can be completely healthy on well balanced, quality dog foods and feeding dogs and puppies large amounts of excess table scraps should be avoided.

Your veterinarian or breeder can help you select a nutritionally balanced puppy food that provides the proper amounts of protein, fat, fiber, vitamins and minerals. There is also a standard you can look for when you're buying puppy food, and that is the AAFCO approval. The stamp of AAFCO, the Association of Animal Feed Control Officials, indicates that the food meets the nutritional requirements for dogs.

Special feeding preferences

For puppies, in general, it is recommended that dogs be fed a quality puppy food because the proper formula, with more nutrients, accommodates the growth needs of rapidly growing puppies.

Veterinarians and responsible, experienced breeders can talk to you about specific breeds in relation to diet. For example, for very large breeds it is often recommended that they not stay on puppy food after a certain number of weeks due to the growth of their large bones.

Feeding schedules

Because of the faster metabolism of young puppies, they can eat up to four times per day. Dog food will have instructions for feeding that are based on age and body weight.

While there are variations in veterinary recommendations, a sample of a schedule for feeding puppies looks like this:

Age of Puppy	Number of Times to Feed Daily
8 to 12 weeks old	3 to 4 times per day
3 to 6 months old	3 times per day
6 months old	2 times per day (some breeds stay at 3x day to 11 months; sometimes it is recommended that you switch to 2 feedings a day when your puppy is 4 months old)
Adults	2 times per day (adult dogs often receive a dog food meal at dinner, and a biscuit or smaller bit of food in the morning)

If your puppy came from a responsible breeder who is staying in touch and advising you, the breeder can give you information based on years of experience related to your breed of puppy's ideal feeding plan and diet.

Something to chew on

Puppies like to chew. When you come home to discover your precious puppy has chewed a big hole in the corner of your favorite chair, you might think you have a behavior problem on your hands. You don't. Chewing is a developmental need. Just as human babies teethe, puppies need to chew to help the teething process.

Chewing can be a real problem however, because when it comes to chewing, it seems that there is a rule that all puppies are born with and that rule is, "Never go for the old worn out flip-flops;

If they don't have enough appropriate chew toys, puppies will find their own things to chew such as furniture, shoes or nice grooming tools.

choose carefully, Young Pup, and chew a nice big piece right out of the toe of the high end high heels. You know—the ones with the red bottoms by the fabulous French footwear designer. And if your human mom doesn't wear high heels, then go for her favorite, most comfortable shoes, the ones that she considers as irreplaceable as an old friend."

To handle the issue of chewing needs, smart owners will provide puppies with acceptable chew toys that have been suggested by your breeder or veterinarian. Other chew toys are fine as long as you are present to observe the puppy to make sure he is simply gnawing on the chew toy as opposed to tearing of chunks and swallowing them. If swallowed, some chew and dental toys can cause serious problems such as intestinal obstructions.

S.T.A.R. Item #2.
Owner receives Responsible Dog Owner's Pledge

The "R" in S.T.A.R. stands for a Responsible owner. The Canine Good Citizen Responsible Dog Owner's Pledge is a key component of the AKC S.T.A.R. Puppy Program too. Responsibility starts the moment you decide to add a new dog or puppy to your family. In your first AKC S.T.A.R. Puppy class, you'll receive a brochure from the instructor that details the S.T.A.R. program and provides a copy of the Responsible Dog Owner's Pledge. During classes, your instructor will cover various items on the Pledge such as the importance of cleaning up after our dogs. In the last class, you'll complete the final steps of the AKC S.T.A.R. Puppy test. You'll fill out your paperwork to send in to request your S.T.A.R. certificate and medal and in doing so you will sign the Responsible Dog Owner's Pledge.

Benefits of taking the pledge

At the beginning of a class (lasting at least six weeks long) in which dog owners and their puppies will train to earn the AKC S.T.A.R.

Puppy award, each dog owner receives a brochure outlining the program including the Responsible Dog Owner's Pledge.

We truly believe that if all dog owners followed the Responsible Dog Owner's Pledge, problems related to dogs in our communities could be eliminated.

If the Pledge were followed, animal control agencies would no longer have to worry about dogs running at large in the community. There would be many fewer dog bites. Dogs who are controlled with fences and leashes are not running at large, and we know that many bites occur when the dog is off of the owner's property.

AKC CGC Responsible Dog Owner's Pledge

I will be responsible for my dog's health needs.

- Routine veterinary care including check-ups and vaccines.
- Adequate nutrition through proper diet; clean water at all times.
- Daily exercise and regular bathing and grooming.

I will be responsible for my dog's safety.

- I will properly control my dog by providing fencing where appropriate, not letting my dog run loose, and using a leash in public.
- I will ensure that my dog has some form of identification when appropriate (which may include collar tags, tattoos, or microchip ID).
- I will provide adequate supervision when my dog and children are together.

I will not allow my dog to infringe on the rights of others.

- I will not allow my dog to run loose in the neighborhood.
- I will not allow my dog to be a nuisance to others by barking while in the yard, in a hotel room, etc.
- I will pick up and properly dispose of my dog's waste in all public areas such as on the grounds of hotels, on sidewalks, parks, etc.
- I will pick up and properly dispose of my dog's waste in wilderness areas, on hiking trails, campgrounds and in off-leash parks.

I will be responsible for my dog's quality of life.

- I understand that basic training is beneficial to all dogs.
- I will give my dog attention and playtime.
- I understand that owning a dog is a commitment in time and caring.

If the Pledge was always followed, there would be a reduction in restrictive legislation and rules pertaining to dogs. When owners fail to clean up after their dogs on hiking trails and in public places like hotels, the first response of government officials and business owners is often to say, "No more dogs."

Finally, if all dogs and puppies were provided with adequate exercise, play time, and training, there would be many fewer canine behavior problems. Some of these problems actually result in dogs being relinquished to shelters for problems that could have been easily solved. The items that make up the Responsible Dog Owner's Pledge are covered in detail in later chapters.

S.T.A.R. Item #3
Owner describes an adequate daily play and exercise plan

During one of the AKC S.T.A.R. Puppy classes, the instructor will ask each student to describe and commit to a daily play and exercise plan for the puppy. This might be accomplished by giving the students a homework assignment where they write the plan and bring it back to class for discussion, or the instructor might simply ask everyone to briefly describe their pup's play and exercise routines as a part of the "Lessons for the Puppy's People" portion of the class.

The "A" in S.T.A.R. stands for "activity" and when we say activity we mean play and exercise. Both of these are absolutely critical for a puppy to be physically, mentally and behaviorally healthy.

Depending on the ages of the puppies in an AKC S.T.A.R. Puppy class, many instructors begin the class by letting the puppies off-leash in a safe area for a supervised play session. Like young children, puppies can learn through play, even if they are not yet developmentally ready for drills aimed at preparing dogs for competition. Puppies can, however, learn basic skills such as sit, down, and come especially when training is a reinforcing activity.

Why play is important
The dictionary defines play as "exercise or activity for amusement or recreation" (http://dictionary.reference.com/browse/play), but for puppies, play means so much more.

Certainly there are times when puppies appear to be simply amusing themselves as they play. But the furry puppy who is having fun while running and chasing a littermate is actually learning new skills. There is a lot going on in this scenario, including mental stimulation, learning to solve problems ("How can I get that stick?"), physical exercise resulting in strengthening of muscles, improved cardiovascular performance, weight control and benefits for digestion. And maybe most importantly, socialization, which in this case is learning to interact appropriately with other puppies.

Socialization and play

There is a significant interrelationship between play, exercise and socialization. Play provides one of the most important and easily accomplished means of socializing your dog. Play behaviors emerge when puppies are between three and twelve weeks old. During the ages of ten to twelve weeks, increasingly sophisticated play behaviors can be seen. Taking advantage of these critical periods will maximize your puppy's ability to learn through play.

Independent play

Taken into the grassy, fenced back yard for fresh air and sunshine, the litter of five-week-old Labrador Retriever puppies is ready to play. A happy little female crosses the yard with a look on her darling face expressing interest in the world around her. She's wandered off from her littermates on an adventure of her own. First, she picks up a leaf and carries it. Then, she finds something even better to hold while prancing, a stick. She drops the stick and picks it up again, tosses it a few inches into the air, and miraculously catches it. She stops, drops the stick, runs a short distance across the yard, stops again, appears to have an idea, and then she takes a few spins as she chases her own tail.

At ten weeks of age, a spaniel puppy in his new home is taken outside for a play and exercise session. In the landscaped back yard, he spots a large bed of liriope, a tall, bushy, soft grass also called border grass. He pounces on his belly into the grass, nearly disappearing with the grass over his head, and then he pounces again, over and over, matching the arc of a dolphin jumping in the ocean. This pup has made a game of surfing in the border grass.

These two puppies provide a good example of play that puppies engage in on their own without other dogs, people or dog toys. This type of play involves the puppy exploring the world and interacting with the environment. Independent play that focuses on interactions with the environment doesn't involve the dog-dog or dog-human social interactions of other types of canine play, but it clearly has benefits that include exercise, problem-solving, building strength, exploring new stimuli, and developing a sense of confidence and curiosity regarding the world in which the puppy lives.

Play begins with puppies exploring the world around them.

Play with littermates

At six weeks of age, a litter of Bernese Mountain Dogs is outside, and these puppies are busy! Carefully supervised by a responsible human, one puppy discovers steps and tries unsuccessfully to climb up the lowest step. His litter sister is lying at the bottom of the step playing with some leaves. A-ha! The aspiring climber figures out that he just needs a boost, and what a better way to get a boost than using your sister's head as a step-stool. Finally, success! Both puppies make a game of going up and down the first step, and then they run off with the sister chasing the brother.

A litter of nine-week-old Whippets is on a fenced hillside. With an extraordinary amount of coordination already, one puppy starts to run up the hill, turns and barks, and the other puppies follow. Back and forth they run, with repeated changes in the leader. One pair of puppies falls to the ground, play growling, barking, rolling around, and showing their tiny teeth in competition and pretend displays of aggression.

As with independent play, playing with littermates provides opportunities for exercise, problem solving, building strength, exploring new stimuli and building confidence. But when a puppy has a chance to play with littermates, the beginnings of socialization with other dogs takes place and there are many other benefits to play activities. Playing with littermates helps puppies learn to assess the body language of another dog and there are chances to expand the dam's early lessons on bite inhibition. Play that involves pretend threats and pretend aggression ("Look how big my teeth are!") teach puppies to interact appropriately with other dogs and develop healthy social behaviors.

Healthy play with littermates involves pretend threats. "Look how big my teeth are!"

Play with dogs other than littermates

Max, a beautiful Vizsla puppy, has gone on a play date to visit Wyn, a well-trained adult Welsh Springer Spaniel. The Vizsla pup approaches the older dog. Wyn does a play bow to signal he's willing to play, then he drops his head and shoulders to the ground indicating that he is no threat to the smaller puppy. Max touches Wyn's nose with his own nose a few times, then drops into a play bow himself, pounces, and the game is on!

This adult Welsh Springer Spaniel lowers his head to play with a Vizsla puppy.

Many owners like to take their dogs to dog parks for meeting and greeting other dogs. Some dog owners also schedule play dates for their dogs. When play sessions are supervised, they can help dogs learn to both read the body language of other dogs and interact appropriately. A dog who lunges on a leash at another dog when out for walk is often a dog who was not socialized properly as a puppy.

In the case of shelter dogs or rescue puppies who may have had a rocky start in life, a systematic plan for socialization around other dogs is in order. Consider starting with one other dog at a time. Bringing an un-socialized dog into a multi-dog play group can be frightening for the dog with limited experience around other dogs.

Always supervise play sessions with new playmates.

Playing with dogs other than littermates helps puppies expand on the social skills started with littermates. Through play, there are improvements with regard to bite inhibition and exercising appropriate restraints when it comes to interacting with other dogs.

10 tips for puppy play groups

1. Instructor and owners should carefully monitor the play activities of dogs in their care.

2. The instructor should be knowledgeable about canine body language.

3. Keep the sessions short.

4. Watch for and remove canine bullies.

5. Remove any dog with aggressive tendencies immediately.

6. Have a separate group for tiny dogs if there are big, active dogs in the group.

7. Don't push it if a dog is shy or doesn't want to play.

8. Have a calm down activity.

9. Teach owners to call their puppy out of the group and reward for coming.

10. If as an instructor, you don't feel comfortable with dogs playing together off-lead, don't allow it.

Play with toys

Balls, soft flying discs such as a Frisbee®, a variety of tug and fetch toys, stuffed animals and squeaky toys are some of the most popular puppy toys. As puppies age, they will begin to use toys in different ways. In the beginning, a tug toy may be simply a durable toy that is carried around like a prized possession. As the puppy gets older, there may actually be some tugging involved.

The development of canine social skills begins in the litter.

Through toy play, it is easy to see some of the genetic make up of specific breeds. The enthusiastic young Golden Retriever puppy who will fetch a ball and bring it back multiple times may be an excellent candidate for future field work.

When you see your puppy or adult dog playing with a toy, there's a lot more than playing going on. Depending on the activity, puppy toys can be used for:

- Mental stimulation if the games played involve problem solving
- To teach instructional commands (such as "Give" or "Find it!")
- To build a foundation for other training later in life (retrieving, obedience, etc.)
- Activities to reduce separation issues when the owner is gone
- Rewards during training- used contingently, dog toys can be one of the most effective positive reinforcers for training
- Breed specific activities (Sporting breeds retrieving, Terriers and squeaky toys)
- Teaching the puppy to release or "give" an object
- Exercise
- Fun
- Bonding

Different types of toys have different purposes

- **Biting toys.** These can help with teething and can be used to teach puppies that they should not mouth or bite people during play, but a toy instead.

- **Balls.** Balls can teach gross motor skills and provide exercise. Puppies can learn the basics of other skills such as the retrieving that can be developed for hunting, obedience competition or other advanced skills.

- **Chew toys.** These are good for teething and are important during developmental changes in dentition, as they strengthen the face and neck muscles.

- **Noise toys.** These toys teach dogs to not be afraid in the presence of unusual sounds, they teach cause/effect—squeeze it to make the sound, and they can be used for practice at locating sounds.

- **Soft toys.** A familiar soft toy provides comfort and familiarity. Many dogs will take their favorite stuffed animal to their bed. Taking a favorite toy along on a trip will make the dog feel more at home.

- **Hard toys with food inside.** These clever toys can keep a dog busy and thus, reduce separation issues.

Interactive toys

Interactive toys are those that the dog manipulates to make something happen. One of the very first interactive dogs for dogs was the Kong®, a rubber beehive shaped toy in which the hollow center can be filled with treats. Dogs can entertain themselves for long periods of time trying to get the treat out of the toy. Since the introduction of the Kong, a number of companies have started to produce interactive toys that range from a basic toy with multiple squeakers to complex canine brain-teaser puzzles that require the dog to manipulate puzzle pieces to find the hidden treat. Interactive toys can be a nice addition to a behavior plan for a puppy who has separation issues.

S.T.A.R. Story

"When I got my puppy, we started a ritual where we sat on the floor every night after dinner and played with toys. I used toys to teach the beginning of the retrieve that would eventually be important in obedience competition and field exercises. Some nights, I'd put my puppy in a sit-stay while I'd hide the toy. Then I would call out, "Find it!" No matter what game we played, I started the sessions by enthusiastically announcing, "It's Puppy Play Time!" My dog is 11 years old now. Every single night, just as I am finishing my dinner, he goes and gets a toy and takes it to the area where we play. The happy, excited look on his sweet face, the face that is growing increasingly white as the years go on, tells me, "It's Puppy Play Time." Playing with toys is one of our most treasured activities together. Eleven years later, my 'puppy' still loves to do this. He initiates Puppy Play Time as an activity every single day. For us, dog toys have built a bond that has lasted a lifetime." -Dr. Jon Bailey, Professor of Psychology

Playing with people: Games to play with your new puppy

When it comes to playing with your puppy, good judgment is a key concept. If children and dogs are playing together, there should be adult supervision and children should be taught to not let things get too rowdy or out of control. Some puppies, depending on their breeds or learning history (e.g., a dog who has not been socialized) may not seem interested in playing. "Play time" for a puppy not at all interested in play might begin with petting or a canine massage. You and your puppy can have Puppy Play Time both indoors and outside with the following games.

Children and puppies should have adult supervision when playing together.

"Find it." For young pups, hide a toy under your hand. When the puppy can find a toy under your hand, make the game more difficult by putting the toy behind your back. When your pup has learned sit-stay, you can hide the toy somewhere in the room. For a well-trained dog, you can hide the toy in a different part of the house or yard and have the dog find it.

"Take it to…." Teach the puppy to hold a toy. Point the puppy in the direction of a family member who is participating in Puppy Play Time. Say, "Take it to Jessica." As you give the verbal cue, Jessica should clap her hands and call the puppy and give enthusiastic praise when the pup arrives with the toy. In the beginning, your helper can be only a few feet away.

"Follow the leader." This is a good game for indoors and outdoors. The puppy can follow you around furniture if space permits. Outside, you can pick up the pace and have the puppy follow as you run in a fenced area.

"Fetch it." As you say, "Fetch it," throw an age appropriate toy (e.g., a small soft toy for a young puppy) a few feet away and let the puppy pick it up. When the puppy picks up the toy, call the pup to come back to you. Gradually increase the distance when your puppy can do this. This game will eventually involve you throwing a ball a long distance outdoors for the dog to fetch it, and the final application of "fetch it" will be for competitive obedience or field dogs or dogs who are trained to help a person with disabilities.

"Give it to me." This game helps prevent resource guarding (food, toys, etc.). As you sit on the floor and play with your puppy, when the puppy has a toy, say, "Give," and hold out your hand. In the beginning, when the puppy is learning the command, you will have to gently take the toy away. As soon as you get the toy, praise the puppy by saying, "Good boy, give!" Continue the play and repeat the give command, each time enthusiastically praising the puppy. Keep the toy for only a few seconds in the beginning and then give it back. If your puppy is reluctant to turn over her toy, you can exchange it for a food treat in early stages of teaching "give."

This game provides the knowledge for your puppy that it is okay to give up a toy, bone, etc. that you request. Some dogs develop a problem called "resource guarding" in which they will guard and sometimes become aggressive if someone tries to take their toys or touch their food. Teaching your puppy to give you an object from an early age prevents this problem.

"Puppy basics—sit, down, stay, come." Hopefully, you're in an AKC S.T.A.R. Puppy class where your puppy is learning the ABC's of being a puppy—sit, down, stay and come. If your pup is already in class and you've been practicing during the day, do something other than this activity during Puppy Play Time. But, if you're not yet in class, during evening play sessions, you can work on teaching your puppy to sit, down, stay and come. We explain how these skills are taught in a later section.

"I've got you now." So that your puppy tolerates grooming later on, it's a good idea to get an early start in an informal activity by touching your pup's ears, feet, and other body parts. You can hold your puppy, or have the puppy laying or sitting beside you as you touch the feet, legs, etc. Keeping this game light-hearted by saying, "I've got your foot" or "I've got your arm" will result in you soon having a puppy who doesn't mind being touched. For example, for puppies who are touch-sensitive when it comes to their feet, start with only touching the foot a few seconds and then reinforcing the puppy with praise and a treat.

"In, out, on, through." This game teaches puppies to follow instructions and get accustomed to different surfaces and situations. Put a box that is low enough and large enough for the puppy to hop into near the puppy and say, "Get in." Teach the puppy to jump in the box when you tell him to do this. For a large puppy such as a Mastiff or Great Dane, you might not have a giant box handy. You can work on teaching behaviors such as, "Paws up," where the puppy needs to step onto a step with the front feet only, or step onto a low platform such as an aerobic exercise step. Your puppy can also be trained to go through a baby tunnel (from a toy store, this is a mini-agility tunnel) in preparation for becoming an agility dog. Outside, you can put a board on blocks and teach your puppy to walk on the low dog walk.

"Come find me." If your puppy will stay in place or you have a helper who can keep the puppy from following you, go around the corner, behind a piece of furniture, or somewhere not too far away where the puppy can't see you. Call out, "Come find me!" Enthusiastically praise the puppy for finding you. You can increase the difficulty of this game by moving farther away, until eventually you can hide in the house, not give a clue by calling the puppy, and have the helper send your dog to find you. At the most advanced level, finding a lost person is what dogs do in the AKC activity called Tracking.

"Tug of war." Most modern trainers simply refer to this old game as "a tug game," or "a game of tug." Whatever you call it, this is the game where the puppy holds on to a rope, fabric, or other tug toy, you pull one way, and the puppy tries to pull the other. There is some controversy associated with playing tug games with dogs. With young puppies, care must be taken not to pull so hard you damage their teeth or cause injuries to young necks and muscles.

Behaviorally, there is some concern that tug games can teach aggression and that with high-arousal dogs, tug games can quickly escalate to an out of control level. If you choose to play a tug game with your puppy, keep a close eye on how your puppy is behaving. Some breeders and canine professionals will advise against tug games for certain breeds or types of dogs. If you play tug with your puppy, you should be able to end the game without the puppy continuing to grab the tug toy, and there should be no signs that your puppy is taking the game too seriously.

"Tricks." There are a number of tricks you can teach your puppy with some of the easier ones being shake (shake 'hands') High-five, speak (if you have a vocal dog it helps), roll over, and spin. There are several good books on teaching tricks that will help you incorporate tricks into your Puppy Play Time.

S.T.A.R. Item #4
Owner and puppy attend at least six classes

The AKC S.T.A.R. Puppy Test requires the puppy and owner attend at least six classes that are taught by an AKC Approved CGC Evaluator. In addition to more traditional training settings, some of the classes may be in the format of a "field trip" where the dogs visit a pet store, community park, etc. While dogs that have not completed a training course may take the Canine Good Citizen Test (the next level after AKC S.T.A.R. Puppy), there are three major reasons that a puppy training class is a required part of the S.T.A.R program:

1. By attending a class at least six weeks long (class is one hour a week with the owner and puppy practicing at home between classes), the instructor can observe the puppy over time for any signs of aggression, behavior problems and to make sure the puppy is on track developmentally.

2. By requiring the puppy attend a class, the owner is in the hands of an instructor who can help with issues related to raising a puppy right, such as housetraining, crate training, etc. Many of the puppies who are relinquished to shelters are given up because of behavior problems that could have been solved if addressed early and if the owner had the assistance of an experienced dog trainer.

3. Even though an owner may have had some experience training other dogs, we believe that a puppy class is extremely important for puppies. By attending a class over the period of several weeks, the puppy is receives the opportunity to socialize with people and other dogs that is absolutely critical for behaviorally healthy development. As explained earlier, the science regarding the need for early socialization is strong.

Choosing the right trainer for you and your puppy
We encourage you to ask any prospective training instructor a number of questions. Examples of questions might include:

- How long have you been training dogs? How long have you trained puppies?
- What kinds of classes do you teach?
- Have you put any titles on your own dogs? Do you have any certifications or training as a dog trainer?
- What dog sports do you participate in or have you participated in?
- What is your basic philosophy of training?
- What kind of equipment will we be using in class (e.g., collars, etc.)?
- Do you use food rewards? Corrections? If so, please tell me about these.
- Are all sizes of puppies together? Do you have play groups?
- Do you know your drop-out rate? How many students finish your S.T.A.R. classes?
- After the beginning class, do many students go on for additional training?

Even after getting your questions answered, visit the puppy class and observe the instructor in action. Here is what you should evaluate:

- The instructor's skill level in teaching humans (adult learners).
- The instructor's knowledge of dogs/puppies.
- The instructor's communication style with students— pleasant, reinforcing vs. bossy and sarcastic.
- Organization of the class. How long on each topic, how many students/puppies?

- Curriculum—does it teach all you want to learn?
- Do the puppies look happy, eager to learn vs. bored or nervous?
- Do the human students look happy, eager to work, or frustrated?
- Instruction is presented and sequenced so that students and dogs are having success.
- Teaching methods—do you spend all the time listening to the instructor talk or is this an active learning class?
- The instructor's ability to handle any behavior problems or student questions.

To find an AKC S.T.A.R. Puppy or CGC trainer near you, see:http://www.akc.org/events/cgc/cgc_bystate.cfm

Class participation and puppy development

In AKC S.T.A.R. Puppy classes, experienced instructors will be watching each week to ensure that puppies are progressing developmentally. Instructors will also provide information to owners about the developmental needs and tendencies of puppies at various stages of development. The owner who says, "My puppy has a behavior problem. He chews everything in sight," can benefit from the instructor's explanation that puppies have a developmental need to chew; chewing is a part of the teething process. The trick is to provide the puppy with plenty of acceptable chewable toys. When an owner says, "My puppy jumps on people to greet them," the instructor can explain that this suggests some training is needed.

Why six weeks?

More than 2000 instructors (who each had at least two years experience teaching classes) responded to an AKC survey question on the preferred length of time for puppy classes. 6.9% of the instructors had four week classes; 5% had five week classes; a dramatic 61.3% felt that the right amount of time for a puppy class was six weeks, and 26.8% taught puppy classes that were six weeks or longer (in most cases, the longer courses were eight weeks). In this survey, 88.1% of the puppy class instructors were teaching classes that lasted six weeks or longer.

In cases where classes were four weeks long, a number of the instructors reported that they shortened classes to reduce student dropout. To counter this, dog training instructors are beginning to implement creative approaches to encourage dog owners to finish classes. One system, open enrollment (also called modules), involves students purchasing a package of a certain number of classes. If students need to miss any classes, they can attend classes at a later date.

Dogs are permitted to begin AKC S.T.A.R. Puppy classes up to the age of one year. In cases where the age of the puppy is not known (such as with rescue or shelter pups), the age of the puppy can be estimated. Your instructor will be able to work with you and your puppy to address problems that arise as your puppy begins to get a little older and consequently, a little more independent.

S.T.A.R. Item #5
Owner brings bag to classes for cleaning up after puppy

We have two primary goals in the AKC S.T.A.R. Puppy program. One is to get the puppy started on the right paw in life, and the other is to teach the puppy's owner how to be a responsible dog owner. The CGC Responsible Dog Owner's Pledge includes the following section that relates to not infringing on the rights of others:

I will not allow my dog to infringe on the rights of others:

- I will not allow my dog to run loose in the neighborhood.
- I will not allow my dog to be a nuisance to others by barking while in the yard, in a hotel room, etc.
- I will pick up and properly dispose of my dog's waste in all public areas such as on the grounds of hotels, on sidewalks, parks, etc.
- I will pick up and properly dispose of my dog's waste in wilderness areas, on hiking trails, campgrounds and in off-leash parks.

While Item #5 relates to being prepared to cleaning up after your puppy in the class room environment in the presence of your instructor, the real intent here is to make cleaning up after you dog a life-long habit in all situations.

Cleaning up after your puppy

What we're talking about here is cleaning up after your puppy when the pup defecates in an inappropriate place such as in a building, or outside at a park, hiking trail or hotel grounds, and so on.

This subject can be an awkward conversation to have with dog owners because, let's face it, what we're talking about here is poop. Yet despite the subject matter, this conversation is incredibly important. When dog owners do not clean up after their dogs, the first thing that happens is usually a restrictive policy or procedure is put into place. Dog droppings on the hiking trails? "That's it! No more dogs on the trails," says the county commission. Dogs dirtying the park where children play? "As of September 1, all dogs will be restricted to the fenced dog park area within the park" say the city officials.

While feces is the major offender here, it goes without saying that responsible owners will also clean up after their dogs if they urinate indoors in a public place.

What's the big deal? Everyone else's dog is doing it

When an irritated dog owner was asked to clean up after her dog at a city park, she said, "What's the big deal? Everyone else's dog does it. And as soon as it rains, it will wash away. It's only recycled dog food and it is biodegradable." She makes two points here. One is everyone else's dog is doing it, and second, it will wash away.

As for "everyone else's dog is doing it" this might remind some people of their mother's saying, "Well, if everyone else jumped off a cliff, would you?" But this age-old sarcastic response isn't really helpful. *What this is really about is assuming a sense of personal responsibility when it comes to our dogs. We can work to educate others, and we can set a good example even if everyone else does not do the right thing.* We can take a lesson from preschool teachers who teach children, "I am in charge of me, and I'm going to do the right thing."

The science of dog waste

The second point the dog owner in the above scenario made was that dog feces are biodegradable and will wash away. The scientists disagree. When left on the ground, canine excrement can make its way into the water table carrying with it the fecal coliform bacteria that can cause intestinal problems in humans. Canine excrement left on the ground in a public park can spread illnesses that including adenovirus, giardia, parvovirus, roundworms and tapeworms to other animals.

How to clean up after your dog

Pooper scooper. There are several methods for cleaning up after your puppy. In a dog training class or at an event, there is a good chance you'll have access to a pooper scooper, a specially designed clean-up tool with a small shovel like device on one end of a large handle and a second tool for pushing the waste onto the scoop. The waste is disposed of in nearby garbage cans.

The common plastic bag. Most of the time, when you're in the community with your puppy, you'll use a plastic bag to clean up your dog's waste. For this reason, AKC S.T.A.R. Puppy instructors have students bring a bag to class. They want to make sure you're ready and will clean up after your own puppy if necessary.

You can use old plastic grocery bags or purchase special bags. There is an AKC S.T.A.R. Puppy bag dispenser (http://www.akc.org/store/detail/index.cfm) that clips on your puppy's leash. Large quantities of replacement bags are readily available at pet supply stores and online.

Develop the habit of putting a cleanup bag in your pocket every time you leave for a walk. Keeping bags near or attached to your puppy's leash will help ensure you're ready for clean-up each time you take your pup for a walk.

There are five easy steps to using a bag to clean up after your puppy:

1. Put your hand inside the bag.

2. Reach down and pick up the waste with your hand in the bag.

3. Turn the bag inside out.

4. Tie a knot in the end. If you have a specialty bag, seal the sticky end.

5. Deposit the bag in the trash.

The poop police

So you're committed to being a responsible dog owner and you clean up after your puppy. But what about the people you see who don't take the time to pick up after their dogs even though there may be clean-up bag dispensers at the entry way to the park? How do you handle or give feedback to these people, the people who are giving other dog owners a bad reputation and putting dogs at risk for losing access to public places?

S.T.A.R. Story
From an AKC S.T.A.R. Puppy Instructor

One summer evening when I was staying at a hotel in Colorado, I decided to put on my jeans and running shoes and go out for some exercise. As I returned to the hotel from a distance, I saw a woman walking her Great Dane in the meticulously manicured lawns next to the building. She was not exercising the dog; he had been taken out for a 'bathroom break.' And sure enough, he did what she wanted him to do—right on the beautifully landscaped grass at the front entry to the hotel. Business complete, the handler turned and began to leave with the dog. "Excuse me," I said. "Are you going to clean that up?" The dog owner spun around, saw me, and said, "Why don't you mind your own business?" How would you handle this?

We presented this true scenario to the readers of the AKC Canine Good Citizen blog, "Citizen Canine" (http://caninegoodcitizen. wordpress.com). We asked readers, many of whom are AKC S.T.A.R.

Puppy class instructors, how they handle it when they see someone not cleaning up after their dogs. One reader said she's discovered if she gives a firm reminder, the person usually responds with telling her to mind her own business (as in the case above). Instead, she says, "Hello, I noticed you must have forgotten your clean-up bags, so let me get one of mine and I will pick it up for you." She wrote to the blog, "Then I pick up the poop from their dog and give them the bag. I think they are in shock and feel bad that someone else is doing something they should be doing. Maybe the next time they'll clean up."

Under normal circumstances, cleaning up after someone else's dog may be a little more than many of us are willing to do, but the polite offer of one of your extra bags may do the trick for the current situation. When you're no longer present to be the conscience some dog owners need, it's not clear if your lesson will have a long-term effect. To have a lasting effect on this human behavior problem, we're adding an increased emphasis on the human end of the leash in AKC S.T.A.R. Puppy and Canine Good Citizen training.

Being responsible

A goal of AKC S.T.A.R. Puppy classes is to teach puppy owners how to be responsible dog owners. Cleaning up dog poop is clearly not one of life's most rewarding activities, but if we want to own dogs, it comes with the territory.

Follow the rules. If you see a sign that says "No Dogs," that means everyone's dog. In a large city where there aren't many bathroom areas for dogs, the landscaping in front of a hotel may be tempting, but finding another place could result in hotel management having a better attitude toward dogs and their owners.

Cleaning up after our dogs will help all dog owners retain the right to have dogs in public places. When some owners fail to pick up dog waste, all dog owners suffer and before you know it, dogs have restricted access to the public places in which there are problems. Walkers, hikers, and people looking for pleasant places for picnics can become extremely vocal about dirty trails and parks.

Responsibility begins with you. On every walk you take with your puppy, you can set a good example for others.

S.T.A.R. Item #6
Owner has obtained some form of ID for the puppy

In the Responsible Dog Owner's Pledge, owners pledge to keep their dogs safe. The section of the Pledge pertaining to safety says:

- I will be responsible for my dog's safety.
- I will properly control my dog by providing fencing where appropriate, not letting my dog run loose, and using a leash in public.
- I will ensure that my dog has some form of identification when appropriate (which may include collar tags, tattoos, or microchip ID).
- I will provide adequate supervision when my dog and children are together.

How dogs get lost
We all love our puppies and we take every precaution to keep them safe. But, sometimes, a dog gets lost through no fault of the owner. Ways that puppies and older dogs are lost or unintentionally separated from their owners include:

1. Accidents happen. Sometimes a front door is left open or someone forgets to close the gate.

2. The puppy as escape artist. Canine Houdinis can figure out how to get over, under or through a fence that the owner was certain was secure.

3. Hurricanes, floods, wildfires. Unpreventable natural disasters happen and dogs get lost or separated from their families. In recent times, Hurricane Katrina was a natural disaster that separated many dogs from their owners and many did not have the identification so they could be reunited.

4. Theft. Who would steal a puppy? Sadly, the AKC CAR National Pet Theft Database shows the number of pet thefts per year is increasing. Most frequently, when dogs are stolen, they have been left in the car or outside in the yard when the owners are away. Some dogs are stolen when owners tie them for a few minutes to go into a store, etc. Other times, owners can cause an unknown, unscrupulous person to steal the dog by giving too much information about it. Dogs are often stolen within minutes of the owner not being present.

5. Improperly fitted collars. If a collar is too loose, particularly if a dog has a neck that is wider than his head, it is possible for dogs to back out of the collar. When this happens in a park or wilderness area, dogs can run into the woods and get lost.

6. Sporting dogs who don't have a reliable recall. Sometimes hunters lose their dogs when the dogs run off to chase prey.

7. Emergency situations can frighten dogs. We heard about an owner who was seriously injured in a car wreck. When emergency workers opened the car door to remove the dog, the panicked puppy jumped from the car and ran into the woods.

Providing your puppy with identification is critical for keeping your puppy safe. The primary forms of identification include: collar tags, tattoos or microchips.

Collar tags
Advantages. Collar tags provide an easily obtainable form of dog identification. Available via order forms online, at your veterinarian's office, or in a machine at a pet store, collar tags are the least expensive method of identification and on most dogs, they are easy to see. If a dog is loose in your neighborhood, a tag with a phone number allows you to return the dog to the owner immediately.

Disadvantages. If the dog loses her collar, the identification is gone. Tags can break off particularly if a plastic tag is old or the dog is very active. In situations where the collar is removed when the dog is in the house, it might happen that the dog is not wearing the collar and tags when the dog slips through the gate unnoticed. Especially for puppies, collars can be safety hazards because there is a chance they can get caught on something. Also, dogs can sometimes chew and ingest the tags. During natural disasters, collars might come off and if the puppy is stolen, the tags can simply be removed and thrown away.

Tattoos

Advantages. Tattoos provide permanent identification. For owners who worry about the insertion of a microchip, a tattoo can provide an acceptable alternative.

Disadvantages. Owners are concerned with the pain or discomfort associated with a canine tattoo and there is no guarantee that a tattoo is unique to a particular dog. If the dog has a lot of fur, once the fur grows back after the dog is tattooed, it may be impossible to see the tattoo easily. Some owners may not feel good about putting a puppy through the process of getting a tattoo. Also, with the growing acceptance and use of microchips, tattoo awareness is diminishing and tattoos are often not looked on as a best practice.

Microchips

About the size of a small grain of rice, microchips are encoded with identification numbers that are unique and cannot be altered. Chips are usually implanted using a needle-like device just under the scruff of the dog's neck.

Advantages. Microchips are a permanent form of identification. They provide a way for stolen dogs to be identified for the verification of ownership. In cases of natural disasters, such as when so many dogs were separated from their owners during Hurricane Katrina, microchips are the tool that can reunite lost dogs with their families. Microchips can be inserted within seconds and they last for the lifetime of the dog. Shelters, rescue organizations and veterinarians scan for chips in order to return found dogs to their owners. Shelters, rescue groups, and breeders can chip puppies so that they already have a method of permanent identification when they go to their new homes. Unlike what happens when some dogs are tattooed, when microchips are inserted, there is very little resistance on the part of the dog. If your dog is found, because you registered the microchip, all of the relevant information is on file including your contact information and veterinarian. AKC's Companion Animal Recovery (CAR) provides 365 days a year, 24 hours per day recovery service if your dog is lost. You will also receive a collar tag with your enrollment confirmation showing your dog's unique ID number and the AKC CAR toll-free number.

Disadvantages. While the cost of chips is extremely low, some dog owners may opt for less expensive collar tags. Infrequently, a microchip might migrate to an area in which they were not originally implanted, however, complications are very rare. Currently, scanners are available that read every type of chip, but some of the older scanners do not read every chip. After microchips are inserted, in order to be truly effective, owners must register the information with a recovery service. When this last step is left up to owners, and the chip is not registered, the recovery service does not have the necessary information for reuniting the dog with the owner.

AKC Companion Animal Recovery (CAR)

An affiliate of the American Kennel Club, AKC Companion Animal Recovery is America's largest not-for-profit pet identification and 24/7 recovery service provider. CAR provides lifetime recovery services for pets who have a microchip, tattoo or collar tag. CAR began in 1995 and, by 2011, more than 400,000 lost pets had been successfully reunited with their families. With a commitment to constant improvement of their services, CAR now has available the "Spotlight" tracking device that couples tracking via GPS technology with the recovery services of AKC CAR. For more information on CAR, see: http://www.akccar.org/

The Spotlight tracking collar uses GPS technology.

S.T.A.R. Story

On the day after Thanksgiving in 2003, Amy Davis took her daughters to get their Christmas photos taken. Knowing they would be back within an hour, they left their nine month old Weimaraner puppy, Jake, in the backyard. In less than 45 minutes, thieves entered the backyard, took Jake, and left only his collar behind. Rewards were offered for Jake's safe return. Heartbroken, Brad and Amy Davis and their children posted signs, filed police reports, contacted shelters and veterinarians, contacted CAR, and kept up a vigilant search for months. Finally, the family gave up hope that their sweet Jake would ever be found.

Fast forward nearly seven years. On September 7, 2010, Phyllis Arsenault, a recovery specialist from AKC Companion Animal Recovery, placed the unbelievable phone call to the Davis family telling them Jake had been found. Rescued by a gentleman who found him running in the road and was worried he would be hit by a car, Jake was dropped off at the Estill County Animal Shelter in Ravenna, Kentucky. He was more than 420 miles away from his home with the Davis family in Michigan. The shelter scanned the microchip, contacted AKC Companion Animal Recovery and before long, Jake was home with his ecstatic family. "We were thrilled to reunite the Davises and Jake after all those years," said Tom Sharp, CEO of AKC CAR. "Jake's homecoming demonstrates how important it is for pet owners to verify their pet's microchip is enrolled in a lifetime pet recovery service like AKC CAR."

What to do if your puppy gets lost

1. Ideally, your puppy has a form of ID that is registered with a recovery service like CAR. Contact the recovery service with the details.

2. Contact your neighbors and get them on the look-out. If your dog is lost in another neighborhood, canvass that area to let people know a dog is missing.

3. Contact your local animal control/shelter and veterinarians. If the puppy has on a tag for vaccines, the person who finds the puppy may call the veterinarian whose name is on the tag. Be sure to tell shelter/animal control staff if your dog has a microchip and provide that serial number. Even better, go to the shelter and ask to look for your pet.

4. Put up flyers with a photo of your puppy. Place these in prominent places in your neighborhood or near where the dog was lost.

5. Contact the media. Get in touch with local radio stations, television and newspapers that cover lost pets. Local dog clubs often have email lists and they will be happy to put the word out that a dog is missing.

If your puppy is stolen

If your puppy is stolen, follow the above suggestions for a lost puppy. In addition, if your dog was stolen, contact the police and file a police report. When you are canvassing the area from which your puppy was stolen, ask people if they saw anything unusual. Sometimes, offering a reward for the return of your puppy will get good results.

Protecting your puppy

While there are several methods that can be used to provide identification for your puppy, the American Kennel Club advocates using a microchip because it provides a permanent form of identification. When a dog has a microchip, if lost, shelters and veterinarians can find the owners. As an additional measure of safety, a tag on your dog's collar with your contact information will help your neighbors get your dog back to you if she escapes from your house or yard and is found in your neighborhood.

If you move or change your phone number, be sure to update your information with your recovery service provider. There are several major benefits of the AKC Companion Animal Recovery service. You can register any brand of microchip (or tattoos or collar tag numbers) and once you enroll your dog, you only pay a one-time fee and the service is good for the life of the dog. When owners are required to pay a recovery service an annual renewal fee, there is a chance that they may forget. Our puppies are members of our families, and providing permanent identification helps ensure that we've done everything possible to keep them safe.

Chapter 5

AKC S.T.A.R. Puppy Test: Puppy Behaviors

The following five skills from the AKC S.T.A.R. Puppy test are related to the puppy's behavior. Your Evaluator will have opportunities during your puppy classes to evaluate your puppy's progress on each of the following behaviors:

7. **Free of aggression toward people during class**

8. **Free of aggression toward other puppies in class**

9. **Tolerates collar or body harness of owner's choice**

10. **Owner can hug or hold puppy (depending on size)**

11. **Puppy allows owner to take away a treat or toy**

S.T.A.R. Item #7
Free of aggression toward people during class

If there is one behavioral issue that can cause a serious problem for a dog, it is dog to people aggression. At the first sign of trouble, if aggressive behaviors are not brought under control, they can get worse and result in a family not feeling safe and surrendering the dog to a shelter. In a perfect world, shelters would have all of the resources necessary to rehabilitate aggressive dogs whose problems were treatable. But sadly, the reality is many shelters simply don't have the resources and further, they are unable take on the liability of placing a dog with a bite history for adoption. Aggression toward people, if not effectively handled as soon as the problem begins, can ultimately result in the death of the dog. With dog bites ranging from a bite that scares a person, to a bite that requires medical treatment to a fatal dog attack, dog to people aggression can obviously have devastating effects on the person involved in an aggressive incident.

Aggression toward people

A benefit of attending AKC S.T.A.R. Puppy classes is that your instructor can observe your puppy for any of the earliest signs of aggression and teach you what to do before there is a serious problem. Aggressive behaviors also include the precursors to physical aggression which may include growling, snarling, lunging and displaying the body language that precedes a bite. By following the earlier suggestions on socialization and attending puppy classes, you can avoid many aggression problems.

Dog trainers and behaviorists have presented a number of methods for categorizing canine aggression that can manifest itself in aggression toward people. Drs. Peter Borchelt and Victoria Voith, Certified Applied Animal Behaviorists, used the following categories:

- Maternal aggression
- Dominance aggression
- Fear related aggression
- Territorial aggression
- Possessive aggression
- Protective aggression
- Pain related aggression
- Punishment aggression

Maternal aggression: Don't touch my babies!

Maternal aggression occurs when a dam engages in aggression such as biting or snapping to protect her puppies. Puppies are often nursing or sleeping in the litter when the mother feels the needs to protect them from people she does not know. While maternal aggression relates more to the dam than it does the future AKC S.T.A.R. puppy, an incident of maternal aggression could be the first time the young puppy witnesses aggression toward humans. To pre-

Keeping a newborn litter in a quiet, protected place will make the dam feel safe.

vent maternal aggression, the dam and whelping box should be kept in a quiet, protected place, and in the very beginning, the only person removing the pups from the whelping box should be someone known to the dam.

Dominance aggression: You aren't the boss of me!

While there are some debates among canine behaviorists about dominance theory in general, there is clearly a form of aggression related to dominance. However, most often, what appears to be dominance aggression is simply a lack of socialization or a need for training. Some dogs will react with aggression (such as lunging and trying to bite) when a person stands over them or directly stares into their eyes. Dogs who have dominance aggression may get aggressive when a person tries to restrain them to put on a collar, for example, or when someone tries to exit a doorway at the same time as the dog. Dominance aggression is not usually seen in young puppies who have received early training and socialization. Frequent exposure to all shapes and sizes of people during the critical period of socialization and afterwards, along with a rich history of positive reinforcement for interacting acceptably with new people, will result in an adult dog who feels comfortable with other people.

Teach your dog to interact with people in the community.

Fear related aggression: I'm afraid—if I growl maybe you'll leave me alone!

With puppies, fear related aggression occurs when the puppy is afraid of something and reacts by biting or snapping. Some dogs who are afraid will run away or attempt to hide. But others lash out with snapping or biting feeling the need to protect themselves. Puppies who have not been exposed to men or children may bite when a man reaches out to pet them, or when a child makes a quick movement. The best solution for fear related aggression is prevention and early socialization with a great deal of exposure to people of all shapes and sizes including examples such as people in hats and flapping rain coats, men with gruff voices, and children with high-pitched voices.

If your puppy has developed a problem, systematic desensitization is the behavioral procedure that can help. Desensitization involves taking baby steps and very gradually getting closer to the person the puppy is afraid of.

S.T.A.R. Story

We rescued a German Shepherd Dog named Lady. Our best guess was that Lady was abused by a male wearing long pants. When my dad wore Bermuda shorts, she was fine. As soon as he put on long pants, she would not go near him. If he forced the issue, she would snap and try to bite. The behavioral solution was to have Dad wear long pants with the legs rolled up. He would play with Lady and feed her small pieces of chicken. Gradually, he rolled down the legs of the pants, a clever use of desensitization. This had to be repeated several different days with different pants and in different locations in the house until Lady was finally calm when Dad wore long pants. Then we were faced with the somewhat awkward job of explaining to our male guests that they needed to start each visit to our house by standing in the yard and rolling up the legs of their pants before entering.

Fear related aggression is often related to unfamiliar grooming routines such as nail clipping or using electric shears. Early exposure to routines that are paired with reinforcement can prevent your puppy from developing fear related aggression.

Territorial aggression: No trespassing on my property!

Territorial aggression manifests itself when a dog protects what he perceives as his territory. Territorial aggression can be toward another animal, or it can be toward a person. A dog who is roaming around an unfenced yard, gets out, chases and then bites a person who is walking down the street in front of his house is probably engaging in territorial aggression. Not being able to read a property deed, this dog is defining his property as the house, the porch in front of the house, the yard in front of the porch and the street in front of the yard. Dogs with territorial aggression may be perfectly fine around people and other animals when on neutral ground i.e., away from their own property.

For handling a puppy who is showing signs of being territorial we suggest the following three steps: 1) make sure your fences and gates are secure—if necessary, you may need a fenced area within a fence; 2) until your puppy responds reliably to commands, teach everyone in the household a safety routine such as putting the dog in a crate or another room before you open the front door to greet someone; and 3) remember that training is essential. Start with AKC S.T.A.R. Puppy, proceed into Canine Good Citizen training, and then continue to train so that your dog is absolutely reliable on the behaviors of sit, down, come and stay.

Possessive aggression: Mine, mine and mine

Seen with the protecting and guarding of possessions, this is the aggression that occurs when someone tries to take one of the dog's toys, handle her food, touch her bed, take her tennis ball—you get the picture. The dog is saying, "This is mine, don't touch it," and if not stopped early, the protecting of possessions can escalate to a dog who will bite.

Dog trainers talk about "resource guarding." Resource guarding is what the dog is doing when it snaps, snarls or bites to keep you away from food or some prized possession. If you see, this you know you are dealing with possessive aggression. Resource guarding is a problem that is often accidentally shaped by owners. The puppy has a toy. The owner wants to look at the toy and reaches for it. The puppy turns away. The owner reaches again for the toy. The puppy growls. The owner gives in. If this happens, then the puppy learns that growling will result in the person keeping their hands off a prized toy. And when growling doesn't do the trick, some dogs escalate to snapping, then biting.

You'll teach your dog to "give" in AKC S.T.A.R. Puppy classes.

Teach your puppy it is ok for you to touch her bed and toys.

In Item #11 of the AKC S.T.A.R. Puppy test Puppy allows owner to take away a treat or toy, we'll talk more about resource guarding and how to prevent it.

Protective aggression: The bodyguard

Protective aggression toward humans usually occurs when a dog perceives that a person is a threat to his owner or a family member. The first signs of protective aggression usually occur when a dog moves out of puppyhood into adulthood (one year or older). A common situation is when a dog lives with a single person, there is a strong bond, and the dog engages in protective behavior when out on walks or when others come into the home. Some dogs will protect the family's children and in some situations (e.g., a potential kidnapper), this could be good. However, if the dog misinterprets what is happening (such as when children are rough-housing), protectiveness could be problematic. The key to preventing out-of-control protective aggression is to provide the puppy with good training and ongoing socialization.

Pain related aggression: OUCH! &%$#!!!

S.T.A.R. Story

A dog owner called with a question about aggression. She described her nine year old Airedale as "the most loving dog in the world." The dog needed a surgery on her ear and she came home with a swollen ear and many sutures. The day after the dog returned home from the surgery, the dog owner's grandchild came to visit. Before the adults could intervene, interested in the sutures, the child reached out and touched the dog's ear. "The most loving dog in the world" bit the child and her upset owner wanted to know if the Airedale would continue to be aggressive.

What happened with the Airedale is an example of pain related aggression. Veterinarians see a lot of this (along with fear related aggression) and it is why they muzzle dogs for certain procedures. If your puppy is in pain, she may bite if you try to touch her. In this case, the aggression is not as much as a behavior problem as it is a need for medical treatment. For any sign of pain, a trip to your veterinarian is warranted.

As for the Airedale, the dog was fine and training was recommended…for the child.

Predatory and punishment behavior

The other two categories of aggression mentioned by Borchelt and Voith are predatory aggression and punishment aggression. Many trainers would argue that predatory behavior (where dogs chase prey) is not aggression because this behavior is hard wired. However, predatory aggression can be a real problem for owners when their dogs view a neighbor's cat or any other moving animal or thing as prey. Punishment aggression is generally a reaction to a harsh correction from an owner or trainer. This is viewed as a owner/trainer problem that needs to be addressed at the human end of the leash.

Escape and avoidance

While escape and avoidance aren't categories of aggression, avoiding a task is a common form of canine resistance that can turn into aggression. The dog doesn't want her nails trimmed. You touch her foot and she growls. You pull your hand back. You touch her foot again and she bites. While some might label this dominance aggression, this might well be a dog who doesn't show any other signs of being dominant. This aggression is related to a specific task. The solution? Early exposure to the task, desensitization if the problem has already developed, and training beginning when the dog is a puppy.

No matter what the category of aggression, most aggression toward people is caused by a lack of socialization, a lack of training or the human doing something that doesn't make a whole lot of sense to the dog. AKC S.T.A.R. Puppy classes are taught by Canine Good Citizen evaluators who have at least two years experience teaching dogs and their people. You'll learn in class to teach your puppy skills such as sit, down and come, but perhaps more importantly, by attending AKC S.T.A.R. classes, you and your puppy will be exposed to great socialization activities.

S.T.A.R. Item #8
Free of aggression toward other puppies in class

A behaviorally healthy puppy will show no signs of aggression (including growling, snapping, biting, displaying aggressive body posture and threatening aggression) in the presence of other dogs and puppies.

S.T.A.R. Story

I was photographing a litter of Bulldog puppies as they played. I noticed that in the midst of all the fun, a puppy would occasionally bite a sibling. The sibling would yip or grumble and the biting immediately stopped. While this might seem like dog to dog aggression, in fact these puppies were quickly learning from each other the important life lesson that it is not acceptable to bite each other with force. –Mary Bloom, Photographer

While dogs who engage in dog to dog aggression aren't usually also aggressive toward humans, aggression toward other dogs or puppies is a serious problem. Using the categories of aggression by canine behaviorists Peter Borchelt and Victoria Voith in Item #7, dog to dog aggression can occur in the situations that follow.

Maternal aggression

A puppy's first experience with dog-to-dog aggression might be when his dam is aggressive toward another dog who she perceives is too close to her puppies. Another situation in which a puppy might experience maternal aggression would be when the puppy is allowed to venture near a litter that he is not a part of while the puppies are with their dam. This curious puppy might be the surprised recipient of the mother dog's clear message, "Back off!" Ideally, when a dam is with her newborn puppies, other dogs are kept at a distance.

These littermates are engaging in healthy play aggression

Dominance aggression

Littermates often engage in healthy 'play aggression' which is normal. Sometimes however, two older puppies may go beyond play aggression and fight with sufficient intensity to cause injury. The best way to handle this is early identification of the problem and then providing training in the presence of other puppies. With a puppy who is starting to have some problems relating to other puppies, the benefit of attending a puppy class is that instructors are skilled at managing the early signs of aggression, and the class setting gives your puppy plenty of opportunities to practice her good manners.

Fear related aggression

When aggression is seen in puppies, fear is commonly the cause. If an unsocialized puppy who is afraid of another dog lashes out with an aggressive display, the other dog might back off, thus removing the fearful stimulus and reinforcing the puppy's aggressive behaviors.

Puppies are afraid of other puppies and dogs when they aren't familiar with them or if they've had a traumatic event related to another dog. Ongoing exposure and opportunities to interact with other puppies ensure that you don't end up with a dog to dog aggression problem. In cases where there is a fear related problem, systematic desensitization is the behavioral procedure that can be used to teach the puppy other dogs are not to be feared.

> ### Spaying and neutering to prevent dog to dog aggression
> Spaying (for females) and neutering (for males) are surgical procedures that make an animal incapable of breeding. There are health benefits of spaying and neutering dogs, and AKC recommends the spaying and neutering of pet dogs. Often, when dogs show signs of aggression toward people or other dogs, neutering is recommended as the solution. If done early enough, this may help prevent aggression problems, but it is important to know that a dog who has developed a reinforcement history related to aggression will not immediately stop being aggressive as the result of spaying or neutering.

Territorial aggression

Protecting one's territory is mostly seen in adult dogs, however, since puppies are participating in AKC S.T.A.R. Puppy classes until they are one year old, there may be some puppies who show signs of territorial aggression toward other dogs who approach the yard, house, crate or other favorite space. Since the puppy is unlikely to be protecting her territory while on neutral turf such as in a puppy class, this problem is best addressed in the setting in which it occurs. There is a greater tendency toward territorial aggression in some breeds, in particular guard breeds. For all breeds and breed types, the benefit of an AKC S.T.A.R. Puppy class is you'll have an experienced instructor who knows canine body language and behavioral procedures and can guide you through addressing your puppy's problem as soon as it starts. Private lessons in the home with an experienced trainer are a good way to handle many behavior problems.

Possession aggression

Sometimes older puppies are possessive when it comes to their toys, bones or favorite objects. When another dog attempts to take the prized tennis ball or soft toy, the puppy might react. In a multiple dog household, make sure that there are adequate toys for all of the dogs, and teach the dogs to respond to a signal from you. Puppies who are housed with other puppies (e.g., kennels or shelters) may become possessive about their food and food dishes.

Protective aggression

Protective aggression occurs between dogs when one dog shows aggression toward another in order to protect a human. Protective aggression is seen more in adult dogs than puppies; puppies are usually in the position of being protected. For a dog who shows signs of protective aggression, training should be provided to teach reliable behaviors such as leave it, sit-stay and down-stay. Further, the dog should have many opportunities to meet other dogs while in the community. Sometimes appearing to protect the owner from an approaching dog, the dog will lunge at another dog while out for a walk. In S.T.A.R. Item #14 Walks on a leash, we'll talk about dogs who lunge at other dogs when on a leash.

In AKC S.T.A.R. Puppy classes, puppies are introduced on leash.

Once again, socialization is the key

You have probably learned by now that at the heart of the AKC S.T.A.R. Puppy program is an emphasis on early socialization for puppies—from the moment you bring them home, and this means socialization with both people and other dogs. Puppies who have not had exposure to other puppies during the critical periods of socialization will have difficulty behaving appropriately around other dogs when they become adults. Puppies who are well socialized grow into dogs who are confident in the presence of people, other animals, and new situations. The AKC S.T.A.R. Puppy program was developed to make sure this happens for the puppy you love.

---

25 activities for socializing your puppy with other dogs to prevent dog to dog aggression

In the litter

1. Puppy plays with littermates-different rooms inside, outside.

2. Puppy and littermates play with toys.

3. Puppy and littermates are together to play with a person.

4. Puppy and littermates given chance to climb on obstacles, explore new area (e.g., yard).

5. Puppy and littermates eat and drink together.

Puppy comes home

6. Puppy goes to the vet and sees dogs in lobby (keep distance until vaccinated).

7. In multi-dog household, puppy plays with other dog, meets cat, etc.

8. Invite a friend with a puppy over for a play date.

9. Invite AKC S.T.A.R. Puppy classmates over for a puppy party.

10. Play date with an adult dog.

AKC S.T.A.R. Puppy class

11. Puppy with veterinarian's approval starts a class.

12. In class, puppies have time together to play (1-2 puppies).

13. In class, larger group of puppies play together (e.g., 5 puppies).

14. Puppy will leave puppy group when owner calls.

15. Puppy plays in a group of puppies with toys available (balls, soft toys, etc.).

16. On leash (once the puppy has learned to walk on a leash), walks by other pups.

17. In class, works near other puppies on sit and down, stays (initial training may be without the distraction of other puppies close by).

18. Greets other puppies at the beginning of class on leash.

AKC S.T.A.R. Puppy instructors all provide opportunities for supervised play.

In the community

19. Meet a friend with a dog the puppy knows, short walk in the park or neighborhood.

20. Dog Meet-Up (assuming puppy's vaccines are complete and these are well-managed; may be more suitable for older puppies).

21. Dog Park (assuming there is not an overwhelming number of dogs, puppy is vaccinated; may be more suitable for older puppies).

22. Dog Walks, Community activities such as parades and special events (e.g, Howl-o-Ween).

23. Puppy goes to the home of another puppy or dog for a play date.

24. Puppy attends a breed relevant activity with other dogs as an observer (e.g., herding for a Border Collie puppy).

25. Go to businesses that allow dogs (e.g., pet supply stores, pet-friendly bistros, home improvement stores, etc).

S.T.A.R. Item #9
Tolerates collar or body harness of owner's choice

Some of the very first pieces of equipment you will purchase for your puppy will include a collar or harness and a leash. Collars, harnesses and leashes are the tools you'll use to both walk your puppy and train her. If you are attending an AKC S.T.A.R. Puppy class, your instructor will advise you on the equipment that she or he prefers for teaching puppy classes.

We hope that AKC S.T.A.R. Puppy, the puppy level of Canine Good Citizen (CGC), is just the beginning of training for you and your puppy. After S.T.A.R., if you take the CGC test, your puppy will need to wear a regular collar (buckle, slip or martingale) or body harness. No head collars or pinch collars are permitted in the CGC test.

But for now, when you're training your puppy in the AKC S.T.A.R. Puppy program, your puppy can wear the collar/harness type of your choice including:

- Collars (buckle, slip, or martingale/limited slip)
- Body harnesses
- Head collars

Collars

Flat buckle collars

Buckle collars for puppies are usually made of nylon and they have metal or plastic fasteners. For safety purposes, there are quick release or "break-away" buckle collars that are designed to unfasten if the dog should get caught in something.

Advantages of buckle collars are that they are easy to put on the puppy and they are thought by most trainers to be humane.

Disadvantages of buckle collars are that if the puppy is not trained, it is possible to pull on the collar (with the leash) and pressure is placed on the puppy's neck. Another common problem we hear about from puppy owners who choose not to use buckle collars is that their puppies can get out of the collar. When a dog has a large neck and smaller head, it is possible to pull out of a buckle collar. This only needs to happen once near a busy street and the owners will be on their way to the nearest pet store to purchase another type of collar.

This puppy is wearing a flat buckle collar.

Slip collars

Slip collars are those with a ring at each end. When put on the dog correctly, as you stand in front of the dog to put the collar over her head, the collar is slipped through the rings and forms a 'p' shape. A 'q' means the collar is backwards.

One of the main advantages of the slip collar is the puppy or dog can not back out of the collar. Owners say this gives them a sense of security, particularly with very active, not yet trained, hard to manage, or very large dogs.

A major disadvantage of slip collars is the potential for dog owners who are not skilled, experienced trainers to abuse or misuse the collars.

It is important to point out that problems with any training tool such as a collar are not the collar itself; it is the act of using the equipment in an abusive, inappropriate manner that is the problem. It is never acceptable to choke a dog or puppy, and systematic training based on sound scientific principles should always be used in place of harsh corrections.

Martingales/Limited slip collars

The martingale (sometimes called a "limited slip") collar can be considered a variation on the slip collar. This collar has a larger fabric or nylon loop that goes around the dog's neck. A smaller loop to which the leash attaches causes the collar to tighten slightly around the dog's neck when it is pulled. This prevents the dog from escaping from the collar, but it does not result in a choking action.

A martingale collar is also called a "limited slip" collar.

Martingale collars provide a good alternative to slip collars in situations where dogs can pull out of a regular slip collar. They keep the dog from escaping, but they are humane and not easy to misuse by unskilled trainers.

Disadvantages of the martingale or limited slip collar would be that new dog owners are generally unfamiliar with them and it is still possible for the untrained dog to pull on the lead while wearing a martingale.

Body harnesses

As a type of equipment routinely used with tracking dogs (those dogs who find lost people, etc.), body harnesses have been around for decades. In recent years, body harnesses have become the equipment of choice for many owners of small dogs who are concerned about a collar pushing on their tiny dog's trachea. Today, there are many choices of popular brand name body harnesses for all sizes of dogs with different functions including no pull, no jump and "easy to control your dog" varieties.

One advantage of body harnesses is that owners who choose them feel good about using them. There is no pressure on the dog's neck for the untrained puppy who pulls hard enough on a neck collar to gag. Some veterinarians recommend body harnesses, especially for small dogs or those with trachea problems.

As with any type of collar, there are disadvantages that come with using body harnesses. With a body harness, there is no control of the dog's head, so the untrained dog may be harder to control in a basic no-frills harness. Dogs who pull, even small dogs such as Dachshunds, can lean into a harness with their chests and pull hard. Another disadvantage is the more complicated the equipment, the more likely the novice dog owner is to have a problem fitting it properly and putting it on a rambunctious, squirming puppy who is excited about going on her walk. And, with some dogs, there is a long "get this thing off me" adaptation period.

Head collars

In the world of dog training, head collars are relatively new equipment. Patented by Robert K. Anderson, DVM, and dog trainer Ruth Foster in 1987, the Gentle Leader® was the first head collar to be widely popular. Now there are a number of brand names, each with its own unique design and characteristics. Basically, a head collar (sometimes called a head halter) resembles the halters worn by horses. The theory behind head collars is if you can control the animal's head, the body follows. Head collars are used more with adult dogs than with young puppies, but since AKC S.T.A.R. Puppy includes pups to one year old, they may be seen in S.T.A.R. classes.

A primary advantage of head collars is that they are excellent management tools. A large, strong, active dog can be easily controlled with a head collar. If the handler is a person with physical issues (e.g., one S.T.A.R. student was an older woman with a recent neck surgery) or a physical disability, the head collar prevents any pulling or dragging that can hurt the person. Because of the instant control they provide, the owner of a dog who is untrained may happily realize that with a head collar, the dog who was previously restricted to his own yard is now able to go for walks in the neighborhood because he can be controlled with the head collar.

One problem with of head collars are that if they are not fitted properly, they can ride up and put pressure on the lower part of the dog's eye. Put your finger under your lower eyelashes and push gently on your eye—you can see that this results in discomfort and distorted vision. If the type of head collar with a strap under the eye is used, it is critical that it is fitted properly. Some dogs also have an adaptation period to head collars, with an initial reaction of pawing at the collar.

A primary disadvantage of head collars is that they are for the most part, management tools. While it is possible to train a dog in a head collar, in many cases the training does not occur and as soon as the head collar is removed, the dog resumes pulling like a sled dog. While a management tool is a great thing to have for certain situations, it does not always result in the building of a strong bond or relationship between the owner and dog that is seen as the result of effective training.

Help! My puppy won't wear a collar!

Most puppies don't mind wearing a collar; it's the first walk with a leash attached to the collar that is the problem. But if your puppy objects to wearing a collar, especially if you're tempted to buy the heavy leather studded collar for your Chihuahua, start with a lightweight collar that is appropriate for puppies.

Start with very short amounts of time, a minute or two at a time if necessary, and then gradually lengthen the time your pup wears his collar. Play with the puppy, go outside and pair the puppy's favorite activities with wearing his collar. Make sure whatever equipment you choose is properly fitted, otherwise, the puppy has a legitimate right to object to wearing it. This applies to all equipment, even doggy seat belts.

My puppy doesn't like her dresses— Now what?

Some puppy owners have no problems with the puppy wearing a collar; they call us and want to know what to do when the puppy doesn't like her dress or his leather motorcycle jacket! The $43 billion dollar pet industry is a testament to the fact that people love their puppies. There are an unlimited selection of jackets, coats, dresses, hats, boots, jewelry and designer outfits just for your dog.

You can teach your puppy to tolerate a car seat belt by starting with short rides.

In cold climate areas with lots of snow and cold rain, canine coats and boots can keep your puppy warm and dry. For dogs who have no hair, health problems related to temperature regulation and/or a thin coat, a sweater may be a good idea. If your puppy resists wearing weather gear or a sweater, use the same principals as getting your dog used to a collar—start slowing and gradually increase the time while making wearing the clothes a reinforcing activity.

For photo opportunities, such as the annual holiday picture, wearing a hat or costume for a few short minutes can be considered a compliance training exercise in which you practice your puppy's sit or down-stay.

But for the most part, if your pup does not want to wear a sailor suit and hat every day, we suggest you listen to your dog. Here are some things to think about when it comes to puppies and clothes:

- Most puppies are already wearing a fur coat and they can get overheated if you expect them to live each day in canine couture.

- Puppies and adult dogs need to have freedom of movement so they can sniff, explore, and make sense of the world around them. That pretty little dress or handsome shirt and pants can restrict movement such as running and playing as well as resulting in safety risks if the clothes are caught on objects.

- Even though your puppy is the cutest puppy the world has ever seen, puppies are canines—they are not babies and they should not be considered as fashion accessories. Puppies need to run through the yard, jump in an attempt to catch a butterfly, roll in the grass, and play. Clothing hampers that experience.

- Finally, and perhaps most important of all, dogs are dogs and they communicate with each other through canine body language. Clothes can hide the signals that one dog sends to another in order to communicate. For photos and the occasional short period of time, enjoy those canine costumes. But most of the time, we hope that you'll choose to enjoy your puppy as dogs are meant to be—without clothes.

Choosing training equipment

When you introduce the puppy's first collar, observe your puppy closely. You may want to consider switching the equipment (e.g., from a body harness to a neck collar) to make the puppy more comfortable especially while he is growing. This might mean getting started on a plan to teach the puppy not to pull in a regular collar. Whatever equipment you choose for your puppy, it should be well fitted and always used in a humane manner. AKC S.T.A.R. Puppy classes have experienced instructors who can help you choose the training equipment that best meets the needs of your puppy.

S.T.A.R. Item #10
Owner can hug or hold puppy (depending on size)

In this AKC S.T.A.R. Puppy exercise, your instructor will watch to see if your puppy tolerates being held or hugged by you. Small dogs can be held in your arms and larger breeds can be hugged. These are the baby steps that lead up to someone other than you, the puppy's owner, being able to examine or handle your dog.

Holding your puppy

Depending on his age and breed, when your puppy is very young there will be many times when you will want to be able to hold and carry your puppy without him putting up a fuss and resisting.

Small puppies

With small puppies, you should be able to:

- Pick up your puppy to rush outside to prevent a housetraining accident.

- Hold your puppy so that others can meet him.

- Carry your puppy when necessary to keep her safe.

- Hold your puppy to put him in a carrier (a carry bag).

Large puppies

We certainly don't expect you to pick up a seven month old Mastiff and put him in a carrying case or carry him up the stairs. For larger breeds, hugging can be used to prepare the puppy for the necessary handling that will occur throughout your dog's life. With both smaller and larger puppies, you should be able to:

- Move around the puppy while you dry him with a towel.

- Practice the types of holding that veterinarians and veterinary technicians will do.

- Prepare any potential therapy dogs by teaching them to accept a hug.

This puppy is comfortable while being held.

10 exercises for holding and hugging

The first step is for you (and your veterinarian) to be able to hug and hold your puppy. Then your family members should be able to do this, then regular visitors to your home along with other puppy class students. The last step is for someone in the community to be able to pet and handle your dog when appropriate. Here is a list of exercises to try to get your puppy comfortable with holding and hugging:

1. Hold your puppy in your arms (if the puppy is small enough).

2. While holding your puppy, pet her.

3. While you are holding your puppy, allow family members to pet her.

4. While holding your puppy, allow someone else (neighbor, someone in class) to pet her. Give the person instructions as to how your puppy likes petting, e.g., "Don't reach over her head; start by petting her on her side."

5. For both large and small puppies: Sit on the floor at home. Put the puppy on your legs. The puppy is lying on your legs, belly-up, and the pup's head is against your body. Some trainers call this the "control position." (For extra large puppies, the puppy can be beside you).

6. While the puppy is sitting or lying on the floor, pet or massage him on the head and chest in a relaxing manner. This activity can be done at home as well as in class.

7. In class, or at home, have people sit in a circle and play "pass the puppy." In class, each owner hands

Teach children in your family how to hold your puppy.

125

their puppy to the next person. Each person keeps the puppy a short time and then passes it to the next person.

8. For older and larger puppies, rather than holding the dog, people can move around the circle in class to pet the dog.

9. Use a towel or brush to introduce grooming exercises while you hold or stand near the puppy. Grooming will be discussed in S.T.A.R. Item #13.

10. As you hold your puppy, eventually move beyond petting and start handling your puppy's ears, mouth, and feet. How to do a brief exam of your puppy will also be discussed in S.T.A.R. Item #13.

Safety first

The exercises above are for younger puppies. In cases where you acquire a dog who is an adolescent, young adult or older adult who has never been handled much, proceed cautiously, especially when it come to handling, petting or hugging by people your dog does not know. The benefit of attending AKC S.T.A.R. Puppy and Canine Good Citizen classes is that an instructor who knows canine body language will be able to help you decide how to work with your dog if there are any behavioral issues with regard to being touched and handled.

Holding and hugging tolerance varies

Dogs are like people—some breeds and individual dogs within breeds are more "touchy feely" than others. While the individual temperaments of socially reserved dogs should be understood and respected, no matter what the breed or breed mix, you should be able to hold and hug your puppy.

Put me down!

What about the young puppy who wiggles, squirms and puts up a ruckus when handled, insisting that you put him down immediately? The key here is to not reinforce resistive behavior. Wait until your puppy is calm to release him.

Don't put me down! Putting your puppy in a carry bag

If you have a small puppy, you should be able to hold her. But this doesn't mean she should be sewn to your sleeve and you should carry her everywhere. For traveling, a carrier is a good option. Some puppies tolerate being held so well that putting them down is the problem. Here is how you can teach your puppy to ride in a carry bag:

1. Choose a carrier that is good for training. Some carry bags have both top and side openings while others only have an opening at one end. If you purchase a carrier with both a side and top opening, you'll be able to teach your puppy to get into the carrier.

2. Make sure the carrier is designed so your puppy will be comfortable. It should be well ventilated and have enough room for your puppy to stand, lie down and turn around.

3. To begin training, place the carrier on the floor. Put a treat near the carrier and tell the puppy, "Get it!"

4. Next, place some treats inside the carrier. Now the puppy has to enter the side opening to get the treats.

5. Practice this on different days for short sessions. The mistake that most dog owners make is buying a carrier, putting the puppy inside, and immediately expecting the puppy to stay in the carrier for an extended period of time.

6. When you need to use the carrier to transport the puppy, make sure you've provided adequate exercise and a chance for the puppy to relieve herself before being confined.

Hugging your puppy: What's love got to do with it?

Hugs are a human thing. Dogs don't hug each other and for that reason, some trainers suggest that hugging a dog is not such a good idea. Their thinking is that while we humans may have good intentions, hugging is certainly not a universally recognized sign of affection in the canine world. There is concern that dogs may perceive hugs as an attempt to dominate them, that bending over a dog for hugging can be misread, and clearly, when you hug a dog, you violate his personal space.

We disagree. As long as a puppy or dog has had the proper training, hugging is a great thing. We love our puppies, hugging makes us happy, and that is precisely why we have puppies in the first place. Hugging can assist with the development of all of the functional skills mentioned above (e.g., tolerating veterinary exams, grooming), and it is a good compliance exercise when training a dog. That said, if the dog have you acquired is an adolescent, adult or puppy with behavior problems or limited training, or a breed that is known to not welcome touch, you should proceed in a systematic fashion to develop very basic "tolerates handling" behaviors before you plunge into hugging.

Some dogs will take all the pets and hugs they can get and they'll gladly take them from anyone. Other dogs are more reserved and as your puppy's advocate, you may have to draw the line and request that people unknown to your dog restrict their greetings to petting. Some people may need a polite reminder that proper canine petting etiquette is that you always ask permission from the owner before petting a dog or puppy. Certainly, it is never appropriate for someone to walk up to an adult dog, lean over and attempt to hug or kiss it.

Therapy dogs

If you plan to go on to therapy work with your puppy, know that "tolerates a restraining hug" is a skill on many therapy dog tests. Therapy organizations know that there are a lot of people who can't resist hugging a dog and many more who are better off as a result.

While this puppy's eyes and mouth say he is not yet comfortable with a restraining hug, tolerating hugs is a part of therapy dog training and testing.

S.T.A.R. Item #11
Puppy allows owner to take away a treat or toy

In this AKC S.T.A.R. Puppy item, your instructor will observe to make sure the puppy will allow you to take away a food treat or a toy. Your puppy can hold onto the food or toy, but he or she should not growl, bite or snap. A behaviorally healthy puppy will trust you. When you're at home, your puppy should permit you to take a toy, touch his bed, pick up his food dish while he's eating or take away a treat.

I can touch your dish...or toy...or bed

If you notice that your puppy is beginning to protect her toys, bed, balls, food and other prized worldly possessions, she is starting to do what animal behaviorists call "resource guarding." We talked about this briefly earlier in S.T.A.R. Item #7. As with many behavior problems, the best solution for resource guarding is prevention and early training to keep the behavior from happening in the first place. If not stopped early, the protecting of possessions can escalate and you may find yourself with a puppy on your hands who is willing to snap or bite rather than give up her stuffed animal.

Since resource guarding is a problem that is often accidentally shaped and reinforced over time, watch for any signs that your puppy is being overly protective of her possessions. Plan activities throughout the day that give you a chance to handle your pup's toys, dishes and bed. If the puppy ever objects by growling, do not give in. This starts you down the dangerous slippery slope of having a puppy who will growl, then snap, then bite to protect her possessions. Why? Because it worked for her!

How to avoid resource guarding

1. Develop your mindset. Start by understanding that basically, you are the human and everything in the house, yard and car belongs to you. It is all on loan to your precious puppy.

2. Life is about give and take. During puppy playtime, occasionally ask your puppy to "Give." Take the toy away for a few seconds. Then give it back and praise the puppy. When you are teaching this skill, you can exchange one chew toy for another, or exchange a toy for a treat. In the beginning, as soon as the puppy releases the item and "gives" as you say the word, give the puppy a treat.

3. Don't let food become an issue. With a puppy, you can start early by handling the food dish and adding something to it so that your puppy learns good things come from you. If you've adopted a shelter or rescue puppy, know that prior to being rescued, these dogs may have been in a situation where they had to guard their food if they wanted to eat. You might need a behavior plan to address food guarding.

4. Compliance training on basic good manners skills will help you address your pup's problems with possessiveness. Sit and down as well as sit-stay and down-stay are all behaviors that can be used to manage your dog while your work on possessiveness issues.

Start handling your puppy's food early to prevent resource guarding.

Safety first: My dog guards his dish

If you have an adolescent or adult dog who is a resource guarder, we believe your best course of action is to get help from a trainer who has experience dealing with this problem. If there are young children in the home, you'll want to make sure that you carefully supervise your dog while he is eating. If the food dish and food have become a problem, one solution is to change the way you feed the dog. Give your dog free access to water at all times, but you should remove the food dish except when feeding the dog. Put your dog's food away. Then, during mealtimes, put the food in a bowl that you hold as you conduct training sessions. Use the food as a contingent reward for complying with your requests to come, sit, down or do other functional skills. Never let anyone tease your puppy with food or toys.

Fighting over food with other dogs

Some dogs, especially dogs from rescue or shelters, get a rough start in life. They may have been in situations where if they wanted to eat, they needed to be prepared to protect their food. These dogs have a learning history that results in them becoming food guarders. Hopefully, you'll get your puppy started on the right path through training and resource guarding will never be an issue for your dog. If your puppy is in a household with other adult dogs, you may not see an issue when your puppy is still young. Puppies have "puppy license" which means that older dogs will often put up with annoying puppy behaviors. When the puppies grow up and become sexually mature, when they're real dogs, then everything changes and they are expected to follow the rules in the canine world.

Food fight!

If you have more than one dog and have problems with them fighting over food, here are some tips follow:

1. Prevent the problem. If your dogs are not yet trained to follow commands and they are having disputes over the dinner bowl, prevent the problem by controlling the environment. If there is a serious problem, don't let a fight happen. Feed the dogs in their crates or in separate rooms. If the food guarding is manageable, feed the dogs with some distance between them. For example, one could be fed at one end of the kitchen, one at the other end, while you stand in the middle.

2. Basic canine table manners. If they don't know the commands already, teach the dogs to come to a specific "Dinnertime!" command. Also teach "Sit" and "Wait" until you say "Okay" (or whatever word you want to use to indicate it is okay to eat the food.) Work on "Sit," "Stay" and "Leave it" until your dog responds reliably to these commands.

3. The Ultimate Dinner Companion. Conduct short training sessions with your dogs together in different areas of the house. Start with a neutral room and eventually work in the area where the dogs eat. Have the dogs sit in front of you, then give each a treat for waiting. For a higher level

of training, work on using their names as you release them one at a time ("Buster, get it!") to take a piece of food.

Resource guarding with people

S.T.A.R. Story

Beau was a large mixed breed dog who passed the required screening so he could go to work with his owner. For the first few days Beau participated in the "Dogs at Work" program, he was well behaved, cheerfully greeting each worker who stopped by his owner's cube to pet him. On Day 4, there was a problem. Beau was sitting near his favorite stuffed animal from home. An employee who stopped to pet Beau every day bent down and picked up the toy to engage Beau in play. Instantly, Beau growled and snapped, as if to issue the firm warning, "Do not touch my toy!"

That was Beau's last day on the job and he no longer came to work with his owner. What happened? Beau had a problem with someone other than his own family members handling his toys. This is the reason that providing your puppy with training that involves interacting with other people and dogs in a variety of contexts is so important. If your puppy has a tendency to be protective of any resources, as an owner, you'll need to be extremely vigilant with regard to telling people how to interact with your dog.

"Give"

Teaching your puppy to "Give" on command was briefly mentioned above. Here are some additional tips on teaching your puppy to give.

1. Set up practice sessions at home. Plan designated practice sessions at home rather than only asking the puppy to give you something when you need or want it.

2. Begin with a neutral toy. To start teaching "Give," the basic idea is you will be taking something your puppy is holding and exchanging it for something you've got. To make the training go faster, don't start by asking the puppy to give you her most favorite toy in the entire world. She is less likely to want to do this, and the point here is to achieve quick success. So, give the puppy something to hold that is fairly neutral.

3. Give the verbal command. When the puppy is holding the neutral toy, say, "Give."

4. Make the exchange. As soon as you say, "Give," take the item the puppy has and quickly give her the item you've got in return.

5. Make the exchange item something good. If a dog had a piece of steak in his mouth and you said, "Give," took the steak and replaced it with a piece of carrot, unless your dog is an unusual salad lover, this system isn't going to work well for you. Start with something fairly neutral and give the dog something great in return such as a favorite toy or treat. Trainers call the something great a "high value reinforcer."

6. Reinforce the giving. You've just said, "Give." As the puppy releases the item, give her the exchange item and say, "Good girl, give!" Eventually, you'll be using praise and phasing out the item exchange when you ask your puppy to give you something.

7. Giving a favorite item. When your puppy is consistent with making the swap of the neutral item for a high value reinforcer, you'll move on to this next phase of training. In this phase, the puppy will have a favorite item, such as a toy. Say, "Give," when the puppy gives you the favorite toy, immediately praise her ("Good girl, give!") and give her a tasty food treat. When she is finished eating the treat, give her toy back. This is the beginning of building trust. If you do this consistently and systematically, eventually your puppy will respond to the verbal cue "Give" with no treats or object exchange.

8. When your puppy will give you a toy or treat on command, you can begin to introduce your family members into the training.

9. Have the puppy play with others (ball play, soft discs, other outside games) and give items. Do this in different settings such as the park, in class, in your yard, in the house.

10. As an advanced exercise, try your hand at the very basics of the obedience retrieve. Throw an object such as a toy, bumper or dumbbell as you say, "Fetch." When your puppy brings the item back, have her sit in front of you and "give" the object.

In AKC S.T.A.R. Puppy classes, you'll practice the "Give" command, with your puppy.

Allowing you to take a take away a treat or toy is an important be-havior because it shows that your puppy does not guard resources. Teaching your puppy to respond to your request to "Give," builds trust and ensures that when necessary, you'll be able to handle any of your puppy's possessions.

Chapter 6

AKC S.T.A.R. Puppy Test: Pre Canine Good Citizen Test Behaviors

This section includes skills that provide the foundation for Canine Good Citizen training.

12. **Allows (in any position) petting by a person other than the owner**

13. **Grooming. The puppy allows owner handling and brief exam (ears, feet)**

14. **Walks on a leash. Puppy follows owner on lead in a straight line for fifteen steps**

15. **Walks by other people. The puppy walks on leash past other people five feet away**

16. **Sits on command. Owner may use a food lure**

17. **Down on command. Owner may use a food lure**

18. **Comes to owner from five feet away when name is called**

19. **Appropriate reaction to distractions when presented fifteen feet away**

20. **Stay on leash with another person as the owner walks ten steps away and returns**

S.T.A.R. Item #12
Allows (in any position) petting by a person other than the owner

With their exceedingly sweet faces, soft fur, large eyes and pure innocence, puppies have a magical, magnetic force that draws people in. People want to look at puppies, get close to them, talk about how cute they are, comment on their attractive characteristics ("Look at the size of those paws!") and they want to pet them.

Tolerating petting is an important skill for all puppies. Without a doubt, the adorable puppy who allows petting makes people incredibly happy. But petting is also a functional, practical skill that lays the foundation for the handling that will later be done by groomers, veterinarians or anyone who needs to handle the puppy in an emergency situation. Puppies who are destined to become therapy dogs will have a career that is largely based on tolerating petting by people other than the owner.

In this AKC S.T.A.R. Puppy test item, the evaluator will observe to see if the puppy allows a petting by someone other than the owner. While squirming and wiggling is acceptable, any signs of aggression are not permitted. Owners may hold small dogs for petting.

Don't pet me!
Dogs are different. Many dogs like petting so much that when a person stops petting them, they will begin to paw at the person to indicate the clear desire for petting to continue. Other dogs are more aloof. Even if allowed, they don't care to sit on the couch with the family or get on the human's bed at night.

Animal behaviorists point out that petting and hugging dogs are something that we as humans brought to the game. Dogs don't pet or hug each other naturally and many don't like hugging, especially restraining hugs. Whether the dog places being petted at the top of her list of favorite activities or not, accepting petting is important because this is the very first step in preparing the puppy for the more intensive handling required when the nails are trimmed and ears are cleaned.

As you work with your puppy on accepting petting from someone other than the owner, make sure you practice with various positions including holding the puppy while someone pets (for small dogs), and petting while the puppy is sitting, laying or standing near the owner.

You'll practice having someone else pet your puppy in S.T.A.R. classes.

Accepting petting: The naturals, the shy puppy and the over exuberant puppy

The naturals

Some pups are born naturals when it comes to social skills and accepting petting. With near perfect social skills from the day they are born, you'd think the naturals read Dale Carnegie's *How to Win Friends and Influence People* while in the womb. While these gregarious, outgoing puppies need ongoing socialization like other puppies, they seem to be dogs who love people and petting from the very beginning.

The shy puppy

Trying to be friendly and eager to meet an irresistible puppy, many people approach and instantly reach out to pet the puppy. Happy and excited, these humans completely overlook the body language of the shy puppy with a fearful look in her eyes that says, "I'm afraid. I have no idea who you are; why are you trying to grab me?"

If a puppy is shy and fearful, the behavioral principle of systematic desensitization will help. As was covered in Chapter 1, desensitization means gradually exposing the puppy to the stimulus that is causing the fear. So, rather than have a person walk up quickly and rapidly pat, pat, pat the puppy on the head, consider using desensitization.

Desensitization steps for a shy puppy

1. Friendly stranger (e.g., a helper in AKC S.T.A.R. Puppy class) walks close to puppy but does not touch him.

2. Stranger approaches, holds out hand, lets puppy sniff hand, but does not attempt to touch the puppy. Another option is to hold a treat, let puppy reach to take it but with no attempt to touch the puppy.

3. Stranger touches puppy, then removes hand. Owner can hold the puppy, with stranger touching the puppy on the back or hip.

4. Stranger pets back or hip. If the puppy is extremely fearful, the owner or stranger can pair treat (such as licking peanut butter) with the petting.

5. Stranger moves hand up body and pets head or under chin.

Tips for teaching the shy puppy to allow petting by someone other than the owner

1. Ask a friend (who will be your training helper) to squat or kneel to the side rather than stand over the puppy. For small dogs, your helper can sit down or sit on the floor.

2. Allow the puppy to approach your helper. Tell your friend not to use a baby voice or reach out for the puppy.

3. When the puppy is close, the helper can hold out his or her hand. When the puppy is comfortable, the helper can pet the puppy.

4. Have your friend use a treat or peanut butter as a distraction if needed (make sure the treats are approved by a vet). As the puppy eats or licks the treat, she can pet the puppy.

The over exuberant puppy

Exuberance when it comes to puppies is a good trait. What we're really talking about here is the *over* exuberant puppy. You might think there is no such thing as being too exuberant for a puppy who loves people and who is

Don't stand over shy puppies for petting.

excited by the world around him. But upon being greeted by a new person, the over exuberant puppy is likely to wag his tail for two seconds before breaking into uncontrollable wiggling which can be accompanied by spinning around and moving near and through your feet like greased lightning. Catching the over exuberant whirling dervish pup in a still moment so you can pet him is harder than catching a fish with your bare hands.

Tips for petting the over exuberant puppy

1. If the puppy's excitement is caused by attention, in a training session, pet the puppy only when he is calm.

2. Consider using distractors such as treats or toys for the young puppy, giving them to the puppy only when he is calm.

3. As the puppy gets older and can learn some skills such as sit and down, teach sit and down-stays. In AKC S.T.A.R. Puppy

classes, you can have helpers (instructors or other dog owners) practice with you and your puppy.

4. The high-on-life over exuberant puppy also needs ongoing, frequent socialization to learn how to behave appropriately for petting from new people.

5. Make sure your puppy is accustomed to being touched. Brushing and canine massage are good exercises for the touch sensitive or over-exuberant puppy.

From accepting petting to Canine Good Citizen

When your puppy reliably allows petting by another person, you can combine AKC S.T.A.R. Puppy Items #12 Allows petting and #16 Sits on command. This will prepare your puppy for the Canine Good Citizen test item Sits politely for petting.

Beyond CGC, advanced forms of tolerating petting are seen in portions of veterinary exams, grooming and in obedience classes where the dog is left in a stand stay with the owner at a distance. A "stranger" (the judge or instructor), walks up to the dog and touches him on the head, shoulders and hindquarters.

The ultimate test for an AKC S.T.A.R. Puppy is politely accepting petting from someone in the community.

Petting, patting and protecting your puppy

There will be times that as your puppy's advocate, you'll need to educate others about how to best interact with your dog. Don't hesitate to do this. Stop screaming school children in their tracks if they are running in a group towards your puppy. Tell them to stop and walk, then show them the proper way to interact with a dog.

When you and your pup encounter an "aggressive patter" turn it into another teachable moment. The aggressive patter is a person who thinks the way dogs should receive petting is to rapidly and repeatedly pat them on the head. Verbal instructions and modeling are the methods of choice for dealing with aggressive patters; you should both *tell* and *show* humans who are clueless how to interact with your dog. *"Her name is Bunny. She is a Cavalier King Charles Spaniel. She isn't so sure about a hand coming over her head. She likes being scratched under her chin. Do it like this."*

Submissive and excitement urination: Whoops!

There might be times when you've reached out to pet a puppy and noticed that the puppy has urinated. Sometimes it is a few drops, and sometimes you need to run for the paper towels.

Submissive urination

With puppies, submissive urination usually happens when someone reaches out to pet the puppy, someone leans over the puppy to pet him, or when an owner returns home and the puppy becomes very excited. While this behavior mainly occurs in puppies, submissive urination can also be a problem for some adult dogs.

This type of urination is associated with dogs or puppies who are very submissive. These are puppies who often squat to urinate or roll over on their sides or show their bellies when greeting an unfamiliar person.

Punishing submissive urination, even if only with a loud verbal reprimand, will make the problem worse. Most puppies will grow out of submissive urination, but some will need a behavioral intervention.

Excitement urination

Excitement urination is different than submissive urination. This occurs when highly excitable dogs lose control of their bladders during activities that involve social stimulation or put them in a state of arousal (i.e., heightened reactions). Excitement urination can occur during very active play.

If your puppy gets excited and urinates when someone new approaches for petting, or you enter a room, here are some tips:

- Never punish this behavior by hitting the puppy or yelling—this will make the problem worse.

- Make sure you give your puppy plenty of socialization and on-going exposure to new people, places and things.

- Identify the stimuli that cause the submissive or excitement urination. Observe very carefully to determine the conditions under which this happens. Trainers refer to the process as a **Functional Assessment** (with a more formal data-based version being the **Functional Analysis**).

  - Is it when a stranger approaches for petting?

  - When you come home after being gone?

  - When you enter a room where the puppy is after she has not seen you for a while

  - When someone stands over the puppy to pet it?

  - When you are playing very active games?

  - When the puppy gets 'wound up' during active play?

Understand the function

Functional analysis is a way of looking at the operant variables that are related to a behavior. Understanding the function of a behavior and the condition under which it occurs can help determine an appropriate solution.

Once you've identified a situation that is clearly a problem, set up training sessions to work on it. Here's an example. Problem: the puppy urinates when people in public walk up quickly and reach out to pet her. What you do: Get a helper to work with you. To begin, this can be a friend or family member and follow this step by step desensitizing approach.

1. Helper slowly approaches up to about ten feet away from puppy and stops. If the puppy did not urinate, go to the next step. At any point the puppy urinates, you need to back up to the previous step. For example, if the puppy urinated when the

person was ten feet away, try this step with the helper fifteen feet away.

2. Helper approaches and gets five feet away from puppy and stops. Did the puppy urinate? If not, repeat this at three feet, then one foot away.

3. The helper is now one foot away. Have the helper hold out her hand and offer the puppy a treat. While the puppy is eating the treat, the helper touches the puppy on the side, then removes her hand. If the puppy is not willing to take food from a stranger, try a toy. You can also use this behavior plan without the treat or toy, but treats are good detractors and often result in faster progress.

4. Helper approaches, offers treat, places hand on puppy and pets.

5. When the puppy can do this with a familiar person, bring in a new helper. Someone from your AKC S.T.A.R. Puppy class would probably be delighted to help you.

6. Vary the places where you do this—at class, in the park, as you take your puppy for a walk in your neighborhood. You can also vary the position of the helper. In the beginning, the person may squat down when close to the puppy and over time remain standing.

Tolerating petting is one of the most important skills for all puppies. Petting is the first basis of other activities that involve touching and handling the puppy. Petting lays the foundation for being examined by a veterinarian, handled by a groomer and meeting people in the community.

S.T.A.R. Item #13
Grooming. The puppy allows owner handling and brief exam (ears, feet)

As the proud owner of a new puppy, you want your puppy to look good. The visible results of grooming, including a shiny coat and well-trimmed nails, makes your puppy look beautiful. But grooming is not only important because you want your puppy to look good, it is also a part of keeping your dog healthy. Your puppy's skin and coat will benefit from being clean and brushed, good nail care is essential and cleaning the ears and teeth can prevent infections that lead to more serious problems.

S.T.A.R. Story

No matter what I tried, I could not get Prissy to allow me to cut her nails. She is a dog I rescued and I don't know what happened to make her so resistive. So, I take Prissy to the vet and let the staff there trim her nails. I don't even go in the room. I know you'll think this is strange, but I teach dog training classes and consider myself a good dog trainer. It's just that for some dogs, this nail-clipping thing is a huge issue. -A frustrated dog owner

Even though you should learn how to do all of the basic grooming tasks related to caring for your puppy, you will likely also want your puppy to tolerate grooming or handling by a veterinarian or groomer should the need arise. The first step in the process is to teach your puppy to allow you to handle his feet and ears as well as allow you to perform other basic grooming tasks.

Hopefully, by the time your puppy comes to live with you, she has been handled and socialized. If she hasn't been handled, your job may be a little harder, but using the AKC S.T.A.R. Puppy program as your guide, you'll be able to get your dog to the point that she looks forward to grooming and being handled.

In this part of the AKC S.T.A.R. Puppy test, the evaluator will check to see if the puppy will allow you to briefly handle the feet and ears. This will better prepare you for the Canine Good Citizen test that follows AKC S.T.A.R. Puppy. In S.T.A.R., your dog has to permit handling by you, and in CGC testing, your dog moves to the next level in which the grooming and exam is done by another person. Your instructor may work on skills that are more advanced than S.T.A.R. in order to prepare your dog for the CGC training that you'll do next.

Exercises to handle your puppy's feet will prepare her for the foot care, nail trimming and grooming that comes later.

A positive approach

There are many puppy books on the market that will tell you about specific shampoos, types of nail clippers and other grooming products. The emphasis in this program is on how to train your puppy and how to handle problems by teaching the necessary skills to solve them. In an area such as grooming, certainly one could wrestle the squirming puppy to the floor and force him to have his nails clipped. The problem with this approach is the puppy can become fearful of grooming and the puppy owner doesn't feel good about doing this. Our goal is to offer an approach based on positive reinforcement and scientifically validated procedures discussed in Chapter 1 such as shaping, fading, chaining and desensitization.

Handling your puppy's ears

As you worked through many of the earlier S.T.A.R. Puppy items that involved your puppy interacting with other people, there have been many opportunities for strangers to handle him. Now we will focus on your puppy learning to tolerate being touched on more sensitive parts of his body. Being able to touch your puppy's ears is the first step to the cleaning and grooming of the ears that keeps your puppy free of parasites and infections. Below is a step by step task analysis that will take you from simply touching the ears to grooming the ears:

1. Touch the ears. Start with simply touching the puppy's ears, one at a time. Don't touch the tips of the ears too lightly or it will tickle and your puppy will twitch or shake his head. If the puppy refuses to have his ears touched, start by touching other parts of his body first. As you touch him, reward him with food for tolerating touch on his side, shoulder and neck. Then move to the ears.

2. Examine the outside of the ears. Once you can touch the ears, hold the ear and feel it, as though you are checking for bumps or scratches.

3. Examine the inside of the ears. After you can feel the outside of the ear, check inside the ears. This is a little more intrusive for a dog with a flap ear such as a spaniel. You'll need to lift the ear and perhaps move hair in order to see inside your puppy's ear.

4. Clean the inside of the ear. You can use clean water or use one of the ear wash products available in pet stores specifically for cleaning ears. Put the water or ear wash on a clean cloth or cotton ball and remove the dirt or wax. Alcohol or mineral oil can also be used to clean dirty ears. This experience will help out in your first veterinary visit when the vet will check your puppy's ears for ear mites, infections and other potential problems.

5. If you've gotten this far, you've gone above and beyond what you'll be doing in your AKC S.T.A.R. Puppy class. This is wonderful progress if you started with a puppy who was resisting being touched. You're on your way to doing the exam required in the Canine Good Citizen test and being able to groom your puppy's ears.

6. The last step is to have someone else check your puppy's ears. AKC S.T.A.R. Puppy instructors will do this exercise in class.

Handling your puppy's feet: That tickles!

Handling your puppy's feet is the first step in being able to care for the nails. Nail care is an area with which many dogs have issue if they have not been desensitized to having their feet handled as puppies. Here is a task analysis that will get you to the point you can trim your puppy's nails.

1. Touch the feet. As with the ears, make sure you don't touch the foot so lightly that it tickles. There were some exercises that focused on this in Item #7, in which the puppy interacted with others. You can do this while you sit on the floor with your puppy for puppy playtime, or you can do this in puppy class. If your puppy won't let you touch her feet, start by touching her side, then move to the upper leg, progress to the lower leg and finally the foot.

2. Examine the feet. When your puppy will allow you to touch each foot, do a small exam—look between the toes and touch and lightly squeeze each nail. This is the step that comes before trimming the nails. If your puppy came to you from a responsible breeder who has already taught the dog to tolerate grooming, consider yourself lucky!

3. Touch the feet and nails with the nail clippers or grinder. A groomer, veterinary technician or your breeder can teach you to use each of these properly. If your puppy resists being touched by the equipment, you can use food as you touch each foot and the dog does not resist.

4. Clip the nails. Holding your puppy and the foot in a secure position, clip the nail. In the beginning, until you get the hang of this, clip only the very tip of the nail, then reward the dog with a treat or praise. Eventually, the food will be faded and nail care will simply be a routine, but for dogs who don't like having their feet handled, a systematic approach can result in a dog who will lay on his side and go to sleep while his nails are clipped and the hair between the pads of his feet is trimmed.

A word of caution about trimming the nails
Make sure you know how to do this before attempting to trim your dog's nails. You're going to clip off (or grind down if you use a grinder) only the tip of the nail. If you go too far, you'll cut the quick, the inner part of the nail containing nerves and blood vessels. In a puppy with white nails, you'll be able to see what looks like a vein in the nail; in puppies with black nails, you can't see this at all, so be careful. Our advice is to get an initial lesson from a groomer, veterinarian, veterinary technician or knowledgeable dog person. Your AKC S.T.A.R. Puppy instructor might also show you how to do this in your class.

Brushing and combing your puppy: Lookin' good!

Brushing and combing your puppy aren't officially a part of Item #13, but since brushing relates to grooming, we'll say a few words about it here.

Brushing is perhaps the easiest part of the grooming routine since many dogs tend to like it and look forward to being brushed. Regular brushing results in a shiny coat and a dog who looks great. This is because brushing removes dead hair and dirt from the coat as well as stimulates oils that make the coat shine.

Choose the brush that is best for your puppy's coat type. Bristle brushes are used on shorter coats, pin brushes are typically used with medium to long coats, and combs are used with dogs who have very short or fine hair. For flat-coated breeds, there is a grooming mitt that looks like a mitten with ridges. When your puppy graduates from AKC S.T.A.R. Puppy and takes the Canine Good Citizen test, the CGC evaluator will brush your dog during the Appearance and Grooming exercise.

Brushing your puppy step by step

1. Show the brush to the puppy. You can put the brush on the floor and let the puppy sniff it, then pick it up and let the puppy smell the brush.

2. Touch the puppy with the brush. If your puppy is afraid of the brush, don't start with brushing his head or face. After showing it to him, touch the brush to the puppy's side or hindquarters. Praise the puppy, "Good boy, get brushed!"

3. Add time to the brushing. You started with only touching the brush to your puppy. Now add a few strokes of brushing. Start with the back end, back legs, and back. If your puppy rolls over, you can brush his belly.

4. Move to the body parts closer to the face. Once your puppy lets you brush his back end (from the middle of the puppy to the tail), brush his chest and front legs.

5. Brush your puppy's head and face, and as a final step, brush the feet. If you have a long coated dog and you're using a pin brush, also get a bristle brush, or use a baby's brush for your puppy's face.

6. Have someone else brush your puppy. This can be family members, a friend, or someone in your puppy class.

If your puppy has come to you from a responsible breeder, chances are he will be a pro at getting brushed. If this is the case, you can skip the baby steps of brushing and get right down to business. Make daily brushing a happy experience for you and your puppy. If you sit on the floor, give the puppy a massage followed by brushing and then puppy play time, before long, you'll have a dog who is bringing you the brush.

Bathing: Rub-a-dub-dub

Bathing is not officially a part of the AKC S.T.A.R. Puppy program, but since you're learning other grooming skills, we'll mention bathing and tooth brushing here so your grooming skills are complete. Here is a step by step plan for bathing:

1. Have the proper equip-
ment.

2. Use a non-slip surface such as a rubber mat so the puppy does not slip in the water.

3. Choose a shampoo that is no-sting so if sham-poo gets in your puppy's eyes she doesn't come to think of bathing as "that thing we do where my eyeballs get burned."

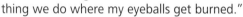

4. Use warm water. Water that is too cold or too hot will make your puppy uncomfortable during bathing.

5. Until she is trained, especially if you are bathing on a raised surface, use a collar and leash to keep your puppy from bailing on you should she decide she's had just about enough of this bath.

6. Finally, while your puppy is learning bathing routines, have some treats ready to reinforce her good behavior.

7. Brush your puppy before bathing to remove any tangles.

8. Wet the puppy and begin shampooing. Some groomers say to start with the head and work back. This is especially true if the dog has fleas. This will prevent fleas from scurrying toward the head of the dog. But, if your puppy has behavioral issues with bathing, you may want to start at the rear of the dog and work forward so the head and face are last.

9. Rinse and dry your puppy. If you use a dryer, take time to get the puppy accustomed to the sound and air coming from the dryer.

Brushing your dog's teeth

If there is one area of canine grooming that is often overlooked, it is a dog's teeth. Brushing is important because it cleans away the plaque that leads to bad breath and more serious problems such as decayed teeth and gum disease.

A dozen tips for dazzling teeth

1. Choose a calm time to brush your dog's teeth. It should be just you and the dog.

2. Buy a canine tooth brush. These are available at pet stores and online pet supply outlets. They have a longer, curved handle that makes it easy to reach the back teeth.

3. Only use toothpaste that is specifically made for dogs. While it works for us, human toothpaste can irritate your dog's stomach.

4. Choose a location for brushing your dog's teeth. The location should have good lighting.

5. Touch the teeth and gums without the brush. Can you do this initial step? Ideally, your dog has been in AKC S.T.A.R. Puppy

and Canine Good Citizen classes and is used to having his mouth handled.

6. Lift the top lip and hold it while you touch the teeth; then pull the bottom lip down and touch the bottom teeth. Touch the toothbrush to the teeth. Touch the front, side and back teeth on the top and bottom. Praise and reward your dog for tolerating this step.

7. Introduce the toothpaste to your dog. Start by showing your dog the toothpaste and letting him lick it from your finger.

8. Add the toothpaste to the toothbrush. Start brushing the top teeth. Hold the upper lip up and brush the front teeth. Be sure to praise your dog.

9. Move from the front teeth further back to the side and back teeth on top. Start brushing the bottom teeth. Hold the bottom lip down and start with the front teeth, then move to the side and back.

10. If your dog is tolerating tooth brushing, you can brush both the outside and inside of the teeth. The inside of the teeth will be a little harder to brush, so if necessary, work on adding this step after your dog is calm with the outsides of the upper and lower teeth being brushed.

11. Getting their teeth brushed is unnatural for dogs. To make this a positive experience, frequently praise your dog.

12. You can also give the dog a treat at each step. This seems counter-intuitive because you are cleaning the teeth and then giving food, but the initial goal is teaching the skill and you can fade the food later.

Many dogs develop an aversion to grooming procedures because someone did not take time to introduce the equipment gradually, the person was untrained and cut the quick of a nail causing the puppy pain, or did not have the proper set-up for bathing so the puppy started to slip and slide in the tub. The positive step by step approach we present in the AKC S.T.A.R. Puppy is designed to make both the puppy and owner feel good about grooming.

S.T.A.R. Item #14
Walks on a leash. Puppy follows owner on lead in a straight line for fifteen steps

When you get your new puppy, one of the very first things you'll want to do is take your puppy for a walk. This means that your puppy will need to wear a collar or harness, and walk along on leash.

"Walks on a leash by following the handler in a straight line for fifteen steps" may seem easy if you have an older puppy and you've already been on walks with your dog. But remember, AKC S.T.A.R. Puppy classes accept very young puppies as soon as their veterinarians give the approval for the pup to be in class, all the way up to those who are one year old when starting class.

This test item meets the needs of the younger puppies, those who within the last few weeks have arrived in their new homes. If you have an older puppy, your instructor will start introducing more advanced exercises to get you and your dog ready for the Canine Good Citizen test.

Walking on a leash

Before practicing walking on a leash, your puppy has already completed AKC S.T.A.R. Item #9 Tolerates a collar or harness. Now you're ready to add the leash and start walking. The idea is to introduce this task to young puppies with some easy steps and eventually make the task harder by requiring the puppy to walk longer distances around other dogs and distractions. You've seen dogs dragging their owners down the street; your goal should be to have your puppy under such good control on the leash that there is always some slack in the leash (forming a 'j' shape). This means you aren't being pulled.

This owner and puppy are doing an excellent job of keeping slack in the leash—note the 'j' in the leash.

Teaching the young puppy to walk on a leash

Decide which side you are going to have your puppy on when you walk. You'll want to keep this consistent and if you don't have a good reason (such as a disability) for doing otherwise, we would suggest teaching your puppy to walk on the left side. If you should get hooked on training and go on to competitive events, you'll need to have your puppy trained to work on your left side as that is the convention in dog showing and training events.

There are several methods for teaching your puppy to walk on leash. This step by step method uses food or a toy to focus the puppy's attention while walking:

1. Identify a toy that your puppy likes or a preferred treat. Before you start walking, you can use the food or toy to play with your puppy and get his attention.

A treat is used to teach this puppy it is rewarding to walk next to his owner.

2. Put the leash on your dog and then start with your puppy at your left side. Hold the leash and toy or treat in your right hand. Hold your hand at the center of your waist.

3. Give the puppy the verbal command to walk such as "Let's walk." (If you have an older puppy and are working on heeling in place, the verbal cue could be, "Heel.")

4. Walk forward, and as the puppy walks along with you, praise him by saying, "Good boy, walk."

5. Every now and then (about every five feet to start), stop and give the puppy a small piece of the food reward or let him play with the toy if he is walking along beside you appropriately. Eventually, you can reduce or fade out the use of food or a toy, and just tell the puppy "Let's walk." If he walks on leash for a longer distance, feel free to give him a treat intermittently. By the time you get to the Canine Good Citizen test, your puppy should be able to walk on a loose lead with no toys or food.

6. Start with five steps, then build up to ten, then fifteen steps in a straight line. Make sure you are going straight and be careful not to step on your puppy's toes.

Building up more distance

Once your puppy can walk in a straight line on the leash as you give encouragement and praise ("watch me, let's go, good boy, walk!"), you're ready to make the task more challenging:

1. Add distance to how far you walk in a straight line. Do away with the training wheels; try having your puppy walk on leash without you holding the toy or food and simply use verbal encouragement and prompts.

2. Add turns. Make a course for yourself (your instructor may do this in class) and add a right turn, left turn and a stop to your walking pattern. This will help you get ready for the Canine Good Citizen test. When you stop, your puppy should stop. Obedience dogs are taught to automatically sit when the owner stops, but this is not required in AKC S.T.A.R. Puppy or CGC. If you are having good success with your older puppy, you can ask your dog to "Sit" when you stop walking.

3. Add circles. After your puppy can make a right and left turn on leash, try adding circles. When your puppy is on your left side, and you make a big circle (six feet in diameter) to the right, the puppy is on the outside and will have to speed up to keep up with you. When your puppy is on the left side and you make a large circle to the left the puppy will be on the inside and will have to slow down to adjust to your pace.

4. Change your speed. Practice walking at a regular pace, then walk fast for small puppies, or run for larger puppies. Your puppy should keep up with you and not get out of control during the fast pace.

5. Walk with your puppy on leash around objects and set up cones or objects so you and your puppy can weave in and out of them.

My puppy is a drag! What to do when your puppy pulls on the leash

This owner makes walking on leash more challenging by picking up the pace.

Puppies are excited about the world. They are eager to get to where they want to go. They want to move on to the next smell, hurry to see a person, rush to a dog that is down the street or move forward with vigor to see what's around the next corner. This unbridled enthusiasm sometimes results in the untrained puppy dragging you down the street. This puppy has got places to go and people to meet and you just happen to be attached to the other end of the leash. If you and your puppy are going to have a long happy life full of wonderful walks together, your dog needs to learn that pulling on the leash is not acceptable. If you give in and allow pulling some of the time, you are reinforcing the wrong behavior (the puppy got what he wanted by getting where he wanted to go faster) and your puppy will continue to pull.

Tips for when your puppy pulls on the leash

1. As soon as your puppy starts to pull on the leash, stop.

2. Don't move. Stand absolutely still. If you have a bigger, stronger puppy, hold on to the leash firmly.

3. Your puppy will pull, but he will eventually stop, so just wait.

4. When your puppy stops pulling, wait a few seconds, then praise and/or reward him with a treat and move forward.

5. Now he's pulling again. You're thinking this didn't work, but have patience. The puppy is still learning how this new game works. If he pulls again, repeat Steps 1 to 4, stop and wait; don't move forward.

6. When the puppy is not pulling, wait a few seconds, praise him, and move forward.

7. The puppy will figure out quickly that he won't be going anywhere as long as he pulls.

8. If you want to move things along a little faster, you can reward the puppy with a food treat when he is walking without pulling on the leash.

S.T.A.R. Item #15
Walks by other people. The puppy walks on leash past people who are five feet away

In AKC S.T.A.R. Item #14, Walks on a leash, your puppy learned to walk in a straight line. Hopefully, you also practiced skills beyond walking in a line such as making turns, circle-right and circle-left and varying your pace. Now it's time to up the ante and get your puppy ready for a walk in the real world. Now you are going to train your puppy to walk on leash by another person. This represents a higher degree of difficulty, especially if your puppy likes to go up and greet everyone he sees. S.T.A.R. Item #15 prepares your puppy for meeting the people in puppy class, your neighborhood and at events that you and your puppy enjoy together.

Learning to ignore other people
The real world has people, plenty of people. Some puppies are afraid of new people or at the other extreme, they want to greet them by jumping up and licking them. And then there are the puppies who sniff people in order to greet them and depending on where they sniff, these puppies might have an embarrassed owner at the end of the leash.

In this test, your instructor will observe to see that your puppy is under control when you walk past people who are five feet away with your puppy on leash. The puppy should not lunge at the people or pull hard to go to a person. The evaluator may allow you to use food or a toy to distract the puppy away from the other people.

Walking past a person who is five feet away is just a starting point. The ultimate goal as your dog learns more skills in Canine Good Citizen training is for you to have a puppy who:

- Permits people to reach out and pet her.
- Walks close to a person or people such as on a busy sidewalk, or for therapy dogs, in the hall of a school or nursing home.
- Walks by people who are standing still.
- Walks by people with different characteristics (tall, short, etc.).
- Walks by other people who have a dog on leash.

Getting started

If you have a young puppy or a dog who has never had any training, the AKC S.T.AR. Puppy goal of walking past people who are five feet away is a great one for you and your puppy to work on. To get started, follow these easy steps:

1. Put your puppy on leash. Have a helper stand about fifteen feet away. Walk past the person with your puppy on leash, coming within five feet of the person. You can praise your puppy and give verbal encouragement such as saying, "Let's go," or "Watch me!" Can your puppy do this? If he

To teach your puppy to pass by another person, start with that person about fifteen feet away.

can, you're ready to check this off your list and move on to a more advanced skill.

2. If your puppy is afraid and balks at the person—or tries to run to him or her—start again by having the helper stand fifteen away. This time walk your puppy past the person at a distance of ten feet away. Can he do this? The idea is that you will pass closer and closer by the person in a systematic fashion. For a puppy who has a problem with this, don't try to walk by a person at a distance of twenty feet and then try just one foot away. Proceed getting closer to the person one foot at a time. For a very social puppy, in early training exercises, you can distract the puppy with food or a toy.

3. When your puppy can walk past a person who is five feet away, make the exercise harder by continuing to reduce the distance and then also circling the person rather than just passing by. First, go around the person in a clockwise circle, then practice doing this counter-clockwise. You'll see that clockwise puts your puppy on the outside with you between the pup and person. Counter-clockwise is a little harder. The puppy is on the inside, walking next to the person. For older puppies, fade the use of food and any distractions such as toys and work on having your puppy reliably pay attention to you when walking past another person.

4. Practice the two distinctly different situations where, on leash: 1) the puppy walks past the person and pays attention to you; and 2) the puppy walks near other people who meet and greet the puppy.

The Akita puppy practices walking by another puppy and owner.

Afraid of people: That person is scary!

S.T.A.R. Story

"I don't know what it is with my ten week old puppy. I've taken her a lot of places and when she gets to know people, she is very friendly. But when we are out, she will meet a new person and try to hide behind me. The person usually talks to her in a very sweet voice and reaches for her to pet her and encourage her to come closer. This just makes it worse. What should I do?"

The first questions you should ask when a puppy appears to be afraid of people is, "How often is she taken out?" and, "How many people has she met?" Most puppies who are fearful of people need more socialization and that is clearly a major benefit of AKC S.T.A.R. Puppy classes.

Start by introducing a puppy who is afraid of people to one new person at a time. Try to shape this behavior by using very small steps to overcome the fear. In class or with a helper at home, have your helper sit on the floor and let the puppy approach. When the puppy will approach a person who is sitting, have the person stand up. The next step is having the person move around. Use a favorite treat and let your helper give the treat to the puppy. Finally, have a helper meet you and your puppy in the neighborhood and give the puppy a treat.

In cases such as in the story above, where the person tried to reach for the puppy and pull her from behind you, remember that you're in charge and need to give well-intended puppy lovers instructions about how they should interact with your puppy. A friendly "Please wait until she is not behind me to pet her," can help.

Another trick for fearful puppies is to teach them an alternative behavior to hiding behind you such as sit (see Item #16, Sits on command). As you get close to the person, instruct the puppy to "Sit," and reinforce sitting as the person comes closer.

Jumping on people to say hello

As you proceed through AKC S.T.A.R. Puppy and into Canine Good Citizen, you'll be working on many things with your puppy and one of them is teaching good manners.

When it comes to having your precious puppy meet another person, good manners means your dog doesn't jump on the person or try to wash their face with puppy kisses. There may be some special circumstances in which a puppy lover invites this, but in general for meeting people out in public, a polite greeting is best.

Jumping solution: Put an incompatible behavior on cue

For the puppy who jumps on people, put another behavior "on cue." This means you will give your dog a verbal cue such as "Let's walk!" and before you pass the person, get the puppy following the "Let's walk" cue. You can also ask your dog to "Sit." Both of these behaviors, when taught reliably, are good for managing an undesirable behavior such as jumping on people because sitting or walking and looking at you are incompatible with jumping up. The behavioral concept here is called "differential reinforcement of an incompatible behavior" (DRI).

Cues, Commands and Instructions

You'll hear trainers say, "give your dog the down command," or "cue your dog to sit." What's the difference between a cue and a command? Nothing really. "Command" was the original term used related to giving a dog a verbal direction to do something such as "Sit," "Down" or "Come."

But, some people feel "command" as related to training dogs has the feel of the trainer dominating the dog or being overly demanding or controlling. For that reason, the word "cue" is becoming more widely used in today's parlance as the term related to giving a dog a verbal direction. Should you choose to talk about cues, what you need to remember is that they can be verbal, sensory or nonverbal such as hand signals. In science, there are even cues related to bacteria.

We prefer the use of the term "command" for a specific instruction like "down on command," since it conveys fairly clearly that this means the dog should follow the handler's voice command. Saying "down on cue," brings up the question, "Is the cue verbal, a hand signal or some other type of cue?" Some trainers will say, "Give the dog the verbal instruction to sit." This is less common and probably less accurate since "instruction" typically relates to teaching. However you choose to describe training your puppy, your training methods should always be kind and humane.

Lunging on a leash

If you've got a problem with your puppy lunging on a leash toward other dogs or people, see S.T.A.R. Item #19 Reaction to distractions.

Sniffing people to say hello

Puppies are busy learning about the world and one way to learn is through scent. So, please excuse the puppy who uses his nose to greet you the same way that dogs greet each other—he hasn't learned good manners yet. It's not personal, but it may embarrass the recipient of the greeting as well as the puppy's owner. When your puppy sniffs people to say hello, call the puppy to you (Item #18 Come when called). Then have the puppy sit or stand-stay to receive a greeting. If you are walking with the puppy, give a verbal cue to remind the puppy, "Let's walk!"

Walks through a crowd: Getting ready for CGC

If you have an older puppy or a super star who has no trouble walking past other people while on leash, start working on getting your dog to do the CGC test item, "Walks Through a Crowd." Here is how to prepare step by step:

1. With your puppy on leash, walk past a person who is five feet away.

2. With your puppy on leash, walk past a person who is one to two feet away. Practice circling this person.

3. Now that your puppy can circle one person, add a second person to your "crowd."

4. Add a third and fourth person to the crowd. In addition to circling and weaving in and out of the people, have people walk toward you and your puppy and pass by as though you were on a crowded, busy sidewalk.

5. Take your puppy to a real sidewalk or activity where there are many people and practice walking through a crowd.

Remember to expose your puppy to different types of people—children, adults, tall and short people, people wearing coats and hats and so on. If you plan on training your puppy to become a therapy dog, start exposing your puppy to people who use wheelchairs, canes or walkers. This can be done in the community or in activities that are set up.

After AKC S.T.A.R. Puppy, Canine Good Citizen grads can work on skills to become therapy dogs.

S.T.A.R. Item #16
Sits on command. Owner may use a food lure

In Item #16, you'll teach your puppy to sit when asked. In the test, your instructor or evaluator will observe as your puppy sits on command. You will be able to use a food lure if your puppy needs it. In this test item, an owner cannot push the puppy into position by pushing on the hips.

Why teach sit?

Sit is one of the first skills most dog owners teach their new dogs. The sit behavior is a relatively easy skill to teach and it is a skill that will be useful throughout your dog's life. Once your dog responds correctly to the "Sit" command, it can be used for practical purposes such as during grooming, when you need to check your puppy's ears, while you wait to cross a street, and as a required skill in other fun dog events such as rally, obedience and agility.

Sit has a second important use and that is as a management tool. A dog who has the problem of jumping up to greet people can be taught to sit and greet Grandma politely. A dog who lunges on a leash at other dogs can be taught a "Sit and watch" procedure that will provide the desensitization the dog needs to other dogs. Whether you're teaching sit as a functional behavior or as a management tool, this is a skill every puppy needs and will use from puppyhood to being a senior dog.

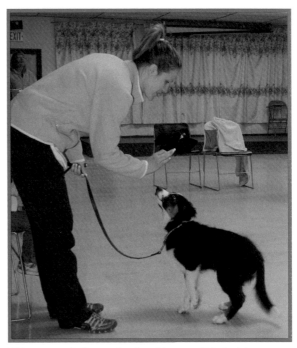

This puppy follows the food lure as it is held above his head and begins to sit.

There are several methods for teaching a puppy to sit. Years ago, a common method for teaching dogs to sit was by saying the word, "Sit" as the trainer physically guided the dog into the sit position. The problem with this technique is there can be a tendency to push down on the dog's hips. This can cause injury and should be avoided.

The method below uses food as a **lure** to guide the dog into position. This beauty of this training technique is that it can be completely "hands off" and force free.

Using a lure to teach sit

1. Select the treat you will use for training. The treat will be used as both a lure (something you use to guide the dog into position) and a positive reinforcer. When you are using food rewards in training, choose a treat that can be given to your puppy in small pieces. Otherwise, your puppy will get filled up quickly and have less interest in training. Also make sure the treat is soft and can be chewed and swallowed easily. You don't want

to use a tough piece of meat, something very hard or something that is very chewy. If you do this, your puppy will have to chew, and chew and chew thereby slowing down training.

2.   Get yourself organized. You want to be able to get your hands on the food reward quickly. You can purchase a treat bag that clips onto your belt, or do this training beside a table or counter where you can place the treats. The benefit of the treat bag is that you'll be able to move around. And, looking like a trainer will help you feel like one!

3.   Get your puppy's attention. Call him to the area where you're going to teach him to sit. Until he learns the skill, minimize the distractions while you're training. Show the puppy the food and get him interested in this. You can give him a piece of the food before the training begins. Trainers call this "reinforcer sampling." Don't do the training right after your puppy has had a meal—he won't be as interested in the food rewards.

4.   Stand in front of your puppy. Let him see that you have another piece of food.

5.   Hold the food in front of and just above your puppy's nose as shown on the previous page. If you hold it too low, she won't see it. If it is too high, the puppy might start jumping to get the food. Most of the time, you'll be holding the food a few inches above the nose.

6.   Begin to move the food toward the back of your puppy's head. At the same time, say, "Sit." Say the word, "Sit" with confidence; this should not be a question that you deliver in a shaky voice, "Sit?"

Praise and reward the puppy immediately when she sits.

7. As your puppy sits (when his rear end touches the floor), praise him by saying, "Good boy!" as you give him the food reward. Eventually, you will just use praise and fade out the food.

8. Repeat Steps 5 through 7 three or four times. By now, your puppy should be starting to sit on his own.

9. Give your puppy a break for a few minutes, then repeat a few more times.

10. Praise your puppy and have a brief play session for a job well done.

What comes next

Once your puppy has learned to sit on command, you can start adding the sit to some of the other skills your puppy has learned.

When your puppy sits on command reliably, you can begin teaching sit-stay at short distances.

- If your puppy is doing well on a leash, practice walking, then stop, and cue the puppy to "Sit." In obedience training, this is called the "automatic sit" once the dog learns that stopping means to sit even if not asked.

- Practice having your puppy sit on command in places other than where you originally trained him to do so. This could include in class, at home, outside, inside, in the yard, on a walk in the neighborhood or in the park, etc. A puppy who sits every time at home probably will need more training to do it in each new location. This is an example of the generalization concept from Chapter 1.

- Fade the food and simply have your puppy sit on command.

- For older and more advanced puppies, start working on teaching sit-stay. A task analysis for teaching sit-stay is below.

Teaching the sit-stay

After your puppy learns a reliable sit, you can begin working on more advanced skills including the sit-stay. Even though this is not on the AKC S.T.A.R. Puppy test, stay will be presented at the next level of training when you and your puppy get to Canine Good Citizen. A sit-stay is a very important skill for your puppy to learn because if he won't stay put after being asked to "Sit," then it can defeat the purpose of the sit. Here is a step by step guide to teaching the sit-stay behavior:

1. Get your food rewards ready. Keep the leash on your puppy if you are training in an outdoor area or your puppy tends to leave the training session indoors.

2. Begin with your puppy sitting at your left side. Move your left hand with the palm facing your puppy's face about six to twelve inches from the puppy's nose. At the same time your hand is in moving in front of the puppy's face, say, "Stay." As you move your hand, make sure your puppy can see your hand signal. Praise your puppy by saying, "Good boy." In this early step, don't move away. Just remain at your puppy's side and reinforce the puppy for remaining in a sit. We're suggesting you use your left hand for the hand signal, but this is a matter of preference. In your classes, your instructor may teach you to use your right hand for the "Stay" command.

3. Pivot to the front of the dog. With the puppy at your side, say "Stay," give the hand signal, and immediately lift your right foot and swing it around to step directly front of the puppy. Bring your left foot to beside your right foot. Praise your puppy by saying, "Good boy."

4. Pivot back into place. Now, reverse the procedure. Step, putting your left foot beside the puppy, and swing your right foot around to its original place. Straighten your left foot so that both of your feet are together and facing front.

5. Gradually increase the distance away from your puppy. Give the "Stay" command and pivot to directly in front of the puppy as you did in Step 4. Now, take one step back so that you're about eighteen inches from your puppy. Praise and reward the puppy for staying. Return to standing right in front of the puppy. *When you get into the finer points of training, you'll learn to step back on your right foot first. Stepping on your right foot*

first indicates to the dog that he is to stay. When your dog is sitting beside you and you step off on your left foot, it is a signal to heel.

6. Repeat the process, each time stepping back a little farther (two steps, three steps, etc.) If your puppy fails, you may be trying to progress too quickly.

Myths about sit

Hounds can't sit. We occasionally get the call from the owner of a hound, usually a Greyhound or a Saluki, and the owner says that the dogs can't sit. Actually, they can sit, it's just that for many of them, par-

ticularly rescue dogs who have not had earlier training, sit may not be the dog's preferred position. In AKC S.T.A.R. Puppy, you'll have it easier because you'll be working with a younger dog and you can use a food lure. Many retired racing Greyhounds have learned to sit so they can compete in obedience, rally and agility. One tip that seems to work well for hounds is to teach the sit from the down position.

A lure is used to teach this Saluki puppy, a Hound, to sit.

Conformation dogs can't sit. *"I can't teach my dog to sit. She is in conformation and if she learns to sit in class, she will sit in the ring."* About six months after we launched the AKC S.T.A.R. Puppy program, we had a photo shoot for some of this country's very first S.T.A.R. grads. The photo session took place at a conformation dog show in Chicago. Two of the puppies who came to have their pictures taken were a Mastiff and a Miniature Pinscher. What a study in contrasts— the giant Mastiff and the tiny little Min Pin. What made the situation more dramatic was these dogs were the exact same age. We had an idea for a photo.

These AKC S.T.A.R. Puppy grads are also winning conformation dogs

If we could get the Mastiff and Min Pin to sit by each other, the photo would make a great ad—"From Min Pins to Mastiffs, puppies everywhere are earning the AKC S.T.A.R. Puppy award!" The owners of the two dogs were willing to give it a try. Within seconds, the Mastiff (a puppy who had already started showing in conformation) was sitting perfectly for the photographer and the Min Pin, posed right in front of the Mastiff, was also doing a perfect down-stay. A dog show judge walked by, saw what was happening, and asked, "How did you get those puppies to sit and lay down like that?" Before any of us could answer, one of the puppy owners proudly replied, "These puppies have graduated from AKC S.T.A.R. Puppy classes. They know how to sit and down on command."

There are many dual ring dogs and they do both conformation and performance events with no trouble. The tricks are to: 1) use different collars/leashes for conformation and events such as obedience; and 2) teach your dog to respond to the words, "Sit," and "Stand." When the conformation dog is in the ring, you can give the command to stand and reinforce stand (conformation handlers are pros at giving food rewards). When you and your dog get to agility, rally or obedience, the dog will be given the cues to sit, down and come on command.

It is possible to have a dual ring dog, all it takes is a little planning and training. And so, there you have it—from Min Pins to Mastiffs, puppies everywhere are learning to sit in AKC S.T.A.R. Puppy classes!

S.T.A.R. Item #17
Down on command. Owner may use a food lure

In Item #17, your instructor or evaluator will observe as your puppy performs a down on command. A food lure may be used. In this test item, owners cannot put the puppy in the position by jerking the front legs out from under the puppy.

Along with sit, the down behavior is an essential skill for every dog. Down can be used in practical situations such as when you want your dog to lay down and take a break, and it can also be used to manage your dog's behavior. Down is an easier behavior for most dogs to maintain than sit, so this is a position in which (when combined with "stay") the dog can relax and rest.

How to teach down on command

This method of teaching down involves using a food lure. The first three steps are identical to the first three steps for teaching sit (see S.T.A.R Item #16).

1. Select the treat you will use for training. The treat will be used as both a lure (something you use to guide the dog into position) and a positive reinforcer. When you are using food rewards in training, choose a treat that can be given to your puppy in small pieces. Otherwise, your puppy will get filled up quickly and have less interest in training. Also make sure the treat is soft and can be chewed and swallowed easily. You don't want to use a tough piece of meat, something very hard, or something that is very chewy. If you do this, your puppy will have to chew, and chew, and chew, thereby slowing down training.

2. Get yourself organized. You want to be able to get your hands on the food reward quickly. You can purchase a treat bag that clips onto your belt, or do this training beside a table or counter where you can place the treats. The benefit of the treat bag is that you'll be able to move around. And, as we said in Step 16, looking like a trainer will help you feel like one!

3. Get your puppy's attention. Call him to the area where you're going to teach him the down. Until he learns the skill, minimize the distractions while you're training. Show the puppy the

food. You can give him a piece of the food before the training begins. Trainers call this *"reinforcer sampling."* Don't do the training right after your puppy has had a meal—he won't be as interested in the food rewards. Make sure you're using a food reward that the puppy really likes and will work for.

4. Start with your puppy in a sit on your left side or stand in front of the puppy. Hold the food in front of your puppy's nose (about a few inches away from the nose).

5. Say, "Down," and as you say the command, move the food in a straight line from in front of your puppy's nose to the ground. The food should end up in front of the puppy's  front feet. Keep your palm down and your hand closed so your puppy doesn't help herself to the food. With a fast dog who may be trying to grab the food, you should move your hand fairly quickly from the nose to the ground. With a slow dog, you can move your hand slower so the dog can follow the food. If you are working with a Toy breed, you can teach the initial Down (and Sit) by putting the dog on a table so you don't have to bend over. Once your puppy can do the skill on the table, you'll practice having him do this off of the table.

6. You've brought the food from the dog's nose to the ground in a straight line so the food is in front of the feet. Now, slide the food out and away from the dog. The whole motion looks like the letter "L." As soon as you say, "Down" and start moving the food to the ground or

floor, most dogs will begin dropping into the down position in order to follow the food. Sometimes they are hunched over. By sliding the food out away from the dog's feet, the dog moves into the down position.

7. The second your puppy is in the down position, praise him by saying, "Good boy, down!" and at the same time, give him the food reward.

Following the lure, the puppy will flatten into the down position.

8. Let your puppy stand up. Get the puppy back on your left side and repeat the steps for teaching down. Do this three to four times, then give the puppy a break.

9. When your puppy is following the command "Down" reliably, you can phase out the food lure, give the command, and reward the puppy at the end with food. Next, fade out the food reward and simply praise your puppy for following the command, "Down."

10. Change positions. Practice having your puppy do down on command with you standing at his side, in front of him, and short distance away. Also practice the down in different places including at home, at training class, in the yard, at the park, and anywhere you are likely to go with your puppy.

Success! A puppy who has learned down on command.

What comes next

Once your puppy has learned to down on command, start adding the down to some of the other skills your puppy has learned.

- If your puppy is walking nicely on a leash, practice walking, take a break, and then cue the puppy to down.

- Fade the food and simply have your puppy down on command.

- For older and more advanced puppies, start working on teaching down-stay. A task analysis for teaching the stay behavior is in Item #16.

- Begin to make down on command a functional skill by teaching your dog to "Go lay down," or "Go to your place." This will involve having a dog bed or carpet where when instructed to lay down, the dog will go to his place and lay down.

Choose your words wisely

Sometimes, when it comes to the idea of "Down," owners confuse their dogs by saying, "Down" when they want the dog to lie down, and they say "Down" when the dog jumps on someone. These are two different behaviors and they need two different commands. "Down" means the dog should drop into the down position. For when your puppy jumps on a visitor, or on the dining room table, use a word such as, "Off!" to prevent any confusion.

Teaching your puppy his name

We're assuming by the time you get to class, your puppy has learned his or her name. You'll use the puppy's name to get attention and give directions, "Bailey, come!"

To teach a puppy his name,

1. Have treats ready and put the pup on leash.

2. When the puppy is looking away, call his name.

3. As soon as he looks at you, give the treat and praise.

4. Wait until the puppy looks away and repeat.

5. Practice this several times a day (until your puppy consistently responds). Then add distances and new locations.

S.T.A.R. Item #18
Comes to owner from five feet when name is called

In this AKC S.T.A.R. Puppy test item, the instructor/evaluator will watch to see that the puppy will come to the owner from five feet when the puppy's name is called. The owner can kneel, clap and make noises to encourage the puppy to come. Food or toys may be used as rewards for coming.

Coming when called is one of the most important skills you will teach your puppy. It is at the heart of nearly everything you do with a dog. You'll call your puppy to come and eat dinner, come outside in a hurry when being housetrained, and come to get her collar so you can go to training class. Perhaps most important of all, when your dog is out in the community, responding reliably to coming when called is a behavior that can save your dog's life.

How to teach come when called

Puppies are generally full of joy and they love to see you. If you have a happy social puppy, you can start with Method 1, the easiest method of all—basically, the technique relates more to the social nature of puppies than it does training. Eventually, the puppy who comes to you every time you call will become a teenager. So while you may find yourself in the seemingly lucky position of not even having to teach this skill in AKC S.T.A.R. Puppy class because your puppy does it on his own, know that sooner or later, you will probably be referring to Method 2.

Method 1

This method involves you making yourself very interesting to the puppy. Kneel down or bend over, clap your hands, make noises or enthusiastically call your puppy. When the puppy gets to you, reward him with praise, petting or a treat. This method works well for young puppies, especially those who don't yet have a mind of their own.

Method 2

1. Get your training materials. You'll need your puppy's collar, a leash (six feet for bigger dogs, four feet for smaller dogs), and food reinforcers.

2. Put your puppy in a sit at your left side. Hopefully, you've also been working on the stay. If not, go back and work on Item #16.

3. Tell your dog to "Stay."

4. As you did when you practiced sit-stay after your puppy learned to sit on command, pivot to stand in front of your dog.

5. Step back one big step. Say "Come." If your puppy does not move to come to you, repeat the cue, "Come," as you give the leash a light tug. You should not be jerking your puppy or doing any harsh corrections.

6. When the puppy comes to you, praise him and give him a food reward.

7. Now walk away from your puppy in *slooowww* motion. When you call your puppy and he comes to you doing what trainers call "the death walk" as though his goal is to walk toward you in slow motion, pick up the pace on your own energy. Run backwards a few steps as you call your puppy with an excited voice.

8. The puppy comes to you, stands in front of you and you praise him. Now you need to practice the skill another time or two. To get your puppy in position, walk him around in a small circle, then set him up again for a sit-stay.

9. When your puppy comes to you when you call him from a few feet away, you're ready to add distance. Go out to the end of your six foot leash and call your puppy.

10. Sometimes call your puppy, other times work on stay. Once your puppy comes to you when called, don't call the puppy to you time after time. If you do that, the puppy will learn that he is always to come to you. Some of the time, practice the sit-stay where you return to the puppy and other times, call him to come.

You can use a very light tug on the leash if your puppy doesn't come when called.

In Method 2, we describe an option of a very gentle tug on a leash when a puppy does not come when called. However, we prefer here that you take the time to figure out why he is not coming to you. Do you need to change your reinforcer to something the puppy likes better? Have you let him ignore your request to come when he is at home off leash, thereby teaching that coming when called is a choice he can make? Do you need to make your training session more fun? If the problem is the puppy is distracted, do you need to do shorter training sessions in a less distracting setting? In some classes, instructors will let distractible dogs work behind a screen until a new behavior is learned.

What comes after coming when called on leash?

- Phase out the food rewards and simply praise your puppy when he comes.

- Add a new behavior; teach your puppy to sit directly in front of you when he comes after being called.

- Extend the distance. In the Canine Good Citizen test, your dog will be required to come to you (on a long line for safety if the test is outdoors) from a distance of ten feet. Practice this once your puppy reliably comes when called from the end of a six foot leash.

Once your puppy comes to you reliably on leash, you can begin to work on coming when called from short distances off leash.

- Eventually, you should work on teaching your dog to come when he is off leash.

- Add distractions during training (see Item #19).

Why won't my dog come when called?

If you go to a park often enough, you're likely to see a frustrated dog owner calling to a dog who is moving quickly in the opposite direction. Why do dogs decide to ignore you and not come when called? There are many reasons including:

- Especially with puppies, if there has not been adequate training, the dog is simply not ready to be off leash. There may be some canine angels who imprinted on the owner early on and they will follow them to the end of the earth. But many puppies get distracted by smells and things they want to see. If your puppy hasn't been taught to come when called (trainers call this skill a "recall"), you can't expect her to do this reliably off leash.

- The puppy's needs aren't met. There will be times when your puppy doesn't come to you because her doggy needs have not been met. She needs to run and exercise, sniff around to find out which dog was here before her, or search for a suitable 'bathroom' location.

- Competing reinforcers. Your sporting dog puppy would really love to please you, but you are taking her for a walk in a field with birds. Let's see…the puppy has a centuries old heritage of flushing birds and she has to make the choice between a sunny, grassy field full of birds and you calling her to come and get a hard, dry dog biscuit as her "reward." Birds-1, Owner-0.

- It's all about you. Sometimes, your puppy won't come when you call him because you have not effectively established yourself as a reinforcer. Your voice is flat, your puppy is excited and full of vigor, but you are slow moving and to a puppy, B-O-R-I-N-G. Pick up your energy level and start having fun with your puppy. Run with your puppy, do fun activities, get on the floor every day for Puppy Play Time and you'll see a world of difference if your puppy is not excited to see you.

- You've provided the puppy with no history of effective reinforcement for coming to you. You call the puppy. He comes. His "reward" is that once he comes, you clip his nails, put him in his crate, clean his teeth, or take him in the house instead of letting him enjoy what he was doing. If most of the time when you call your puppy it is to do something that is not especially fun, the puppy will start to avoid coming when called. The solution? Make yourself the most reinforcing thing in your puppy's world.

If your puppy runs away from you, whatever you do, never call the puppy to you and then punish her. It is nearly one-trial learning where the puppy learns, "If she says, 'Come,' and I go to her, there's a good chance I'm going to be in a whole heap of trouble. I think I'll just keep on running."

If you've done training and made yourself a reinforcer, before long your puppy will happily come when called in any setting.

Coming when called is perhaps the most important skill you will teach your puppy. Coming when called is a functional behavior that you'll rely on throughout the day to manage your puppy's daily routines. Coming when called is also the behavior that can save your dog's life in an emergency situation.

S.T.A.R. Item #19
Appropriate reactions to distractions presented fifteen feet away

In AKC S.T.A.R. Puppy Item #15, you taught your puppy to walk on leash. If walking on a leash was always done in a quiet, controlled environment, going for a walk with your puppy would be easy. But the world is not always quiet and controlled. When out for a walk, you and your puppy are likely to encounter loud noises, objects that move, people with characteristics the puppy has never seen and one of the biggest distractions of all for a puppy—another dog.

Distractions are stimuli in the world your puppy may react to. They include people, other animals, sounds, sights, smells and many other things. When humans talk about distractions, we often think of them as things that take us away from our work or the task at hand. For example, loud music playing in the office next door may be a distraction for someone who is trying to focus on entering data into the computer.

For your puppy, distractions are any number of things that take the puppy's attention from what you are trying to do, such as teaching a new skill or walking down the street. A leaf falling off a tree can be a distraction during training for a sporting dog who responds to subtle, slight movements, and a squirrel running across the park can be a distraction for a terrier breed puppy who is out for a walk. Types of distractions include visual, auditory (sound), scent (smell), motion, people and animal distractions.

In AKC S.T.A.R. Puppy class, puppies will practice skills in the presence of many distractions.

Visual distractions

Visual distractions are those that the puppy sees. They divert the puppy's attention away from the task at hand. Sometimes, the reaction of the puppy to a visual distraction is simple curiosity; other times the puppy may be afraid or it can cause him to want to chase someone or something.

S.T.A.R. Story

I took my Gordon Setter puppy in the yard to practice what she was learning in her training class. I thought she was looking off in the distance to ignore me. Then I realized my puppy was watching leaves that were falling from the neighbor's tree across the street.

Every day, I take my 6 months old Shih-Tzu, Teddy, for a walk. We walk down the street in the same direction and the view is basically the same. But last week, just as we rounded a corner, there was something new. We left home a little early so there was a very large garbage truck in the street that Teddy had never seen before. Have you ever seen a Shih-Tzu levitate? Teddy went straight up in the air and then, he would not stop looking at the garbage truck. It was hard to get him to pay attention to me.

The real world is full of distractions.

Auditory distractions

Auditory distractions are distractions that the puppy hears. Pans or books that are dropped, people laughing, musical instruments, television and radio sounds, tea kettle whistles, fire truck sirens, running water and birds chirping are sounds that can be auditory distractions.

If your puppy jumps out of his skin when he hears a loud noise (e.g., a book drops), practice working with him in the presence of noise distractions. There are plenty of these at dog training classes. When you are trying to get her to pay attention to you, if the problem is your puppy is being distracted by paying attention to noises in the environment that are continuous (e.g., the sound of a radio), work with your puppy to teach her to focus on you. You can use a treat or toy to teach your dog to respond to, "Watch me!"

Teaching "Watch me!"

"Watch me" is the behavior related to getting your dog's attention, and paying attention is critical for your dog to learn new skills. To teach "Watch me," there are a few easy steps:

1. Begin with your dog in front of you. The dog should be close enough that you can easily give him a food reward.

2. Call your dog's name.

3. The second she looks and has eye contact with you, say, "Good watch me!" and give her the food reward.

4. Wait until he is looking off in another direction and repeat the request, "Watch me!" Again, the second she has eye contact, give her the food reward.

If you have a dog who does not look at you or have eye contact when you call her name, you may need to add another step. Start with your dog in front of you. Show her the food. As she looks at the food, move it toward your face. As soon as your dog looks at you, give her the food.

Scent distractions

Because dogs have a sense of smell so much better than ours (e.g., dogs have used their sense of smell to identify cancer in humans), their reactions to smell might be difficult for us to comprehend. You're walking through the park with your puppy and suddenly, he slams on his brakes and begins to sniff. Maybe it was a female dog, maybe it was a possum; you'll never know who or what he is responding to, but there's a good chance your puppy does. Other dogs, small animals, or scents on a person (e.g., the smell of the hamburger you ate for lunch, perfume) can distract your dog from a task. Some of the time on walks, you'll want to give your puppy a chance to stop and sniff; other times, you can give her the cue, "Let's walk!"

Plenty of scent distractions are encountered on walks.

Motion distractions

Teenagers on skateboards, joggers, cars, someone pulling a crate dolly, carts, balls, moving wheelchairs, and other animals are all examples of distractions that can capture your puppy's attention because they involve movement. Certain types of dogs including Sighthounds, Herding and Sporting dogs are highly sensitive to movement. These dogs have a history that goes back centuries of being bred to respond to things that move such as rabbits, birds or sheep. Trainers talk about dogs who are high prey-drive dogs. These are the dogs such as those mentioned above who are wired to chase things that move.

Handling problems related to motion distractions

I'm having a problem with my German Shepherd puppy. He is not trying to kill birds. He is not trying to kill squirrels. He is trying to kill my vacuum cleaner. I want to keep my house clean and I need to vacuum. What can I do?

1. Begin with the vacuum cleaner turned off. Is your puppy okay with it sitting in the room? If not, desensitize the puppy to the vacuum cleaner's presence (see Chapter 1).

2. Sound check. Turn on the vacuum cleaner, but don't move it. Is the puppy chasing it? Most likely, the sound is not the problem, it will be the motion that is the issue. If the puppy is responding to the sound, you should work with the puppy on leash on easy tasks such as sit, down, and walking around the vacuum cleaner. Reward the puppy for "Watch me," behaviors and following commands such as sit and down. Do not give a treat if the puppy is barking at or lunging toward the vacuum cleaner.

3. A moving vacuum cleaner. For this step you need a helper. With your puppy on leash, have the helper begin to move the vacuum cleaner very slowly. Give your puppy the instruction to "Watch me," and reward her for watching. Then, turn off the vacuum cleaner.

Some dogs react to distractions that move.

4. Repeat Step 3 above, and get a little closer to the vacuum cleaner. Gradually get closer and then repeat all steps with your helper moving the vacuum cleaner a little bit faster.

> **Another option for vacuum cleaner attackers**
> Another option if you have an older puppy who has learned a reliable sit-stay or down-stay is to use what is called a "sit-and-watch" procedure. Across the room from where you'll start vacuuming, put your dog in a sit-stay. In the beginning, only vacuum for a few seconds, then go and reward the dog. Repeat the vacuuming, each time adding time to the sit-stay. Sit-stay and down-stay are good management techniques for moving distractions because they stop the dog's momentum and decrease the chance the dog will chase.

Slow down that squirrel!

The vacuum cleaner is a motion distraction for which you can get a helper, slow down the vacuum cleaner and work in small steps. However, this isn't possible if the distraction is a squirrel, a car, or a teenager on a skateboard. You can't tell a squirrel to repeat what it just did, only this time, a little slower please. In these cases, the solution is teaching your puppy AKC S.T.A.R. Puppy and Canine Good Citizen skills so that they are rock solid, then using the skills (such as sit-stay) to put the puppy's behavior on cue.

People distractions

People come in all shapes and sizes. When a puppy sees or hears something he's not seen before such as a gruff voice, a person wearing a long plastic raincoat, or a shrieking child, he may be distracted or afraid. In Item #7, we presented exercises for exposing your puppy to a variety of people.

Animal distractions: Reaction to a distraction dog

Animals can also be distractions for your puppy. One of distractions you and your pup are most likely to encounter is another dog. Some puppies are interested in other dogs and will want to pull you on the leash so they can go and see them. Other puppies, if they haven't had much exposure to other dogs, may be fearful, or worse, aggressive toward other dogs. In the Canine Good Citizen test, one of the items is "Reaction to Another Dog." In this CGC test item, two handlers approach each other with their dogs on leash. The handlers stop, shake hands, and continue on. It may be a while before you and your puppy are ready for CGC, but you can start working on teaching your puppy to respond appropriately when you see another dog.

Other dogs provide distractions.

Puppy pulls to other dogs

My mixed-breed puppy is a great little dog. He loves people. He also loves other dogs, and that's the problem. He is so social that when we see a dog on the street, he wants to pull me over to the other dog. If I let him "go say hello," the next thing I know, he is jumping on the other dog with happiness, the leashes are getting tangled up, and the other dog's owner doesn't look happy.

There will be times, particularly if you have a younger puppy, when your puppy should be given the chance to socialize and play with other dogs. But, when you're out in the community, it is not always appropriate for your dog to initiate play. If your puppy is dragging you to meet another dog, here are some tips.

1. Give your puppy the rules. As you see another dog approaching, tell your puppy, "Let's walk," ("heel" if you have an older pup who has learned this) or "Watch me."

2. Only move toward the other dog when your puppy is not pulling or lunging. If your puppy is pulling toward the other dog, turn around and go in the opposite direction of the other dog. The puppy will learn you are not going anywhere if she continues to pull.

3. Sit-and-watch. If you have an older puppy who has a fairly reliable sit-stay, you can have your puppy sit-stay as the other dog walks by. Praise and reward your puppy for staying in the sit-stay and watching you.

After your puppy learns to walk past another dog and remain under control, if you are in a situation where you want your puppy to greet the other dog (and the other dog owner is open to this) tell your puppy, "Go say hello," or another similar command. Your puppy can learn that there are times when we need to walk along, and other times we can stop and meet a new dog.

Sample distraction exercises for AKC S.T.A.R. puppy classes

Start with each distraction at fifteen feet away, then move it to ten feet, then five feet away from the handler and puppy.

People

- Person moving around
- Person swing a shopping bag
- Child jumping up and down
- Child making a noise
- Person in a funny hat
- Person in a coat
- Person with a walker/wheelchair

Auditory

- Drop a book
- Drop a metal pan
- Bell
- Bicycle horn
- I-Phone sounds
- Whistle

Motion

- Broom (sweeping)
- Wagon
- Skateboard

- Person on bike
- Cars (walk on leash outside)

Advanced

- Walk other dog by puppy on leash
- Walk another puppy by puppy on leash
- People in a line, puppy (on leash) weaves in and out of the line
- Person walks by with balloons
- Person bounces tennis ball, throws toy in air

The environment around us is full of stimuli that are distracting, particularly for a puppy who is learning about the world. With training, your puppy will learn to be confident and unflappable in the presence of any type of distraction.

S.T.A.R. Item #20
Stays on leash with another person as the owner walks away ten steps and returns

When you spend quality time with your puppy and do training activities together, you'll build a bond that is unlike any other. You'll begin to understand your puppy and your puppy will understand you, and if you're like many other people who love their dogs, the world will feel right when you are your puppy are together.

But, as much fun as you have together, there will be times when you'll need to leave your puppy at home unattended or times when someone else needs to take your puppy to provide grooming or veterinary care. Some puppies have problems when they are separated from their owners. In the extreme form, these problems can manifest themselves as separation anxiety.

The purpose of this AKC S.T.A.R. Puppy Item is to begin to teach your puppy that there are times when you'll need to leave and there is no need to panic or become upset. In class, the evaluator or instructor will have you hand your puppy's leash to another person. You'll walk ten steps away and then return to your puppy. Your puppy can show mild signs of distress, such as a little bit of whining, but there should be no extreme reactions.

In your puppy class, you may have already done activities like the game "Pass the Puppy" where owners sit in a circle and, when given a signal from the instructor, each puppy is passed to the next person. Activities like this will prepare your puppy for being separated from you outside the classroom.

Teaching your puppy to stay with another person

To teach your young puppy to tolerate staying with another person while you walk away, proceed slowly. If you have an older puppy and your dog does this exercise with no trouble, you can work on advanced skills.

1. Start by standing next to the person while you hold your puppy's leash.

2. Let the other person hold your puppy's leash. That person can talk to your puppy, offer a treat and pet the puppy.

3. While the other person is holding your puppy's leash and interacting with your puppy, step away one step, then immediately return to stand near your puppy and the other person.

4. Next, take two steps away from your puppy and return. The other person can continue to interact with your puppy in a cheerful manner and offer treats.

5. Take three steps away and return. You will continue training in this manner, adding one step at a time until you can go ten steps and return. If at any time your puppy appears stressed, begins to whine or frantically pull at the leash to come with you, go back to the previous step.

In AKC S.T.A.R. classes, your puppy will stay with another person while you walk away and return.

Beyond Item #20: Going further away

1. When your puppy can do Item #20 successfully, continue to add steps until you can get to the doorway without your puppy reacting.

2. Add the verbal command "Wait." At this point, when you leave the puppy, say "Wait" or whatever command you've chosen to use every time you leave. This command should not be "Stay" which means "stay in the position in which I left you." The "Wait" command lets the puppy know that you will be back.

3. Step outside the door, and immediately return. When you advance to Canine Good Citizen, your puppy will work on CGC Item #10, Supervised Separation. In this exercise, you'll be asked to leave the room for three minutes while someone holds your dog on leash. To begin preparing for this, once you've mastered AKC S.T.A.R. Puppy Item #20, start leaving the room for one second, then three seconds, then ten seconds, and so on, until you can leave your puppy with someone for three minutes.

The most advanced version of leaving your puppy for most of us is when we leave to go to work all day. When you first get your puppy, arrange to get the puppy when you have a few days to establish routines.

Practice going out the door, them coming in. Then you should leave, stay gone a few minutes at a time, gradually extending the time. Use a crate if necessary to keep your puppy safe.

Our puppies should be able to rest and feel comfortable when we're gone.

Problems with leaving your puppy

Whenever puppies have a problem with this exercise, it is usually because owners are proceeding too quickly. If your puppy is having trouble when you walk away, you may need to spend a few practice sessions going only one or two steps away and returning.

When you return to your puppy after having walked away ten steps, if your puppy jumps up and down with joy and acts like you've been gone for 40 years, whatever you do, don't feed into this. It is certainly flattering to have anyone, a puppy included, act as though seeing us is the most exciting thing in the world. But, if you hug or coo over the puppy when he is jumping for joy upon your return from the long journey that took you five feet away, you will teach the puppy that you leaving is a horrible thing. If your puppy is hysterical with happiness as you walk back to him, don't react. Wait until he is calm to calmly praise him.

Reactions to the owner leaving

When dogs have separation issues, there are several types of reactions they can have when the owner leaves them. Some of these include excessive barking, chewing and destroying objects, and urinating or defecating in the house even though they are housetrained.

S.T.A.R. Story

A Noisy Night

One would think that after a night in a nice hotel, I would feel rested today. But, I am beyond exhausted. Last night when I was checking in, I met a woman with four adorable Maltese in the hotel lobby. Wouldn't you know it! Her room was next to mine. She went out for the evening and stayed out until very late. Those dogs barked the whole time.

Seek and Destroy

I would love to give my Staffordshire Bull Terrier the freedom to have the run of the house when I'm at work. I use a crate but would rather not. My dog is well behaved when I am home, but when I leave, he seems to get very upset. When I say upset, I mean if he is not left in his crate, there's a good chance a large part of the stuffing from the furniture will be on the floor when I get home. Or, he will look around and find something that belongs to me and tear it apart.

He's Housetrained

My Dalmatian is housetrained, but when I leave home he will urinate in my bedroom. He's not simply marking the furniture; he will get in the bed or chair and leave a large puddle.

The scenarios above all came to AKC's Canine Good Citizen department from owners whose dogs had issues related to being separated from their owners.

Separation anxiety

Probably the most common term used to describe problems related to owners leaving their dogs is "separation anxiety." Because not all dogs who have problems related to being left alone are experiencing anxiety, animal behaviorists and trainers are beginning to use other terms including separation distress and separation behaviors.

Technically, anxiety is a clinical term that means there are measurable physiological changes in the dog (or other animal) such as increases in blood pressure, heart rate heart palpitations and shortness of breath. In a case such as the one above with the dogs barking in the hotel room, we don't really know that the dogs had "anxiety." The guests in the surrounding rooms probably had migraine headaches and increases in their blood pressure, but there is some chance that the dogs were just barking.

If your dog truly has separation anxiety, you should seek the services of a qualified animal behaviorist or veterinary behaviorist. Sometimes separation anxiety becomes so severe that dogs will try to go through glass windows or they will break their teeth trying to escape a crate. While crate training is often recommended for dogs who have separation behaviors (such as chewing objects when the owner is gone), dogs with separation anxiety can injure themselves in a crate. Behavioral treatment is needed for these dogs.

Separation distress

Distress is the dog's inability to adapt to stress or the conditions causing the stress such as the owner leaving the puppy. Barking, whining, crying, destruction (chewing) and inappropriate urinating and defecating are behaviors that are often the result of separation distress.

Separation behaviors

In the case of the Dalmatian above, there's a good chance that the behavior was related to stress and the owner leaving. But sometimes, what the dog is doing could just be engaging in a behavior that happens when the owner leaves without there being any anxiety, stress, or distress involved. The Staffordshire Bull Terrier could have been stressed when the owner left, and a bona-fide bout of clinical anxiety led to him destroying the couch. On the other hand, this could have also been a dog left with no toys who was simply bored and found an activity that entertained him. The owner reported that the dog was "upset" while she was gone. She assumed this when she saw the furniture torn apart. However, in the absence of additional data (such as a video from while she was gone), we don't know if when the owner was away, this pup was having a nervous breakdown or a party. This is the reason that there are times when behaviorists use the term "separation behaviors."

Home alone: Five tips for leaving your puppy alone

1. Shaping, shaping, always shaping. Proceed systematically one step at a time whether you are briefly going into the next room or leaving the house.

2. Access to toys. Leave your puppy with things to do when you are gone. There are interactive toys that give the puppy something to do and provide an acceptable activity that involves chewing.

3. Meet the puppy's physical needs. Anytime you leave the puppy, think of how you'd like to be treated. Make sure you take the puppy outside for a bathroom break and exercise before you leave. Exercise will help the puppy relax.

4. Develop a consistent routine. Each time you leave, be consistent; do the same thing so the puppy will learn you are going to return. For example, give the puppy a biscuit and say, "Watch the house," as you leave.

5. Always have a calm return. A calm return and greeting lets your puppy know that your leaving was not a big deal, and you always come back.

While you are still training your puppy, in order to keep your puppy safe (and to protect your possessions), crate training your puppy might be a good idea. Some tips for crate training were presented in Chapter 3.

You can learn to crate train your puppy in AKC S.T.A.R. Puppy classes.

Chapter 7

After AKC S.T.A.R. Puppy
What Comes Next?

We're hoping that you and your puppy enjoyed AKC S.T.A.R. Puppy training so much that you're ready to move on to other exciting AKC activities. This section provides a brief description of these activities. For more information, all you need to do is go to www.akc.org and type the name of the activity the in search box.

Canine Good Citizen

We hope that you enjoyed training your puppy. AKC S.T.A.R. Puppy is the puppy level of Canine Good Citizen and CGC is the next step of training for you and your dog. In Canine Good Citizen, you'll work on polishing the skills that you learned in S.T.A.R. by adding time and extended distances to skills. For information on the Canine Good Citizen Program, see: http://www.akc.org/events/cgc/index.cfm.

We consider AKC S.T.A.R. Puppy and Canine Good Citizen warm, friendly introductions to many other exciting training activities that AKC has for you and your dog. The most common activities that dog owners move into right after CGC are Rally, Obedience or Agility. Some enthusiastic owners get hooked on training and do them all! In 2011, AKC added a new title, AKC Therapy Dog (the ThD) and therapy work is also an excellent activity to follow CGC. If you've got a puppy who is ready to compete in activities such as Rally, Obedience or Agility before completing Canine Good Citizen, this is permitted.

For Rally, Obedience, and Agility, we are thrilled to say that both purebred and mixed breed dogs can compete. If your dog does not have an AKC registration number or "papers" (e.g., a rescue or shelter dog),

all you need to do is enroll in AKC's PAL (Purebred Alternative Listing) Program or AKC Canine Partners.

PAL: Purebred Alternative Listing

PAL (formerly called ILP) is a program that allows unregistered purebred dogs of AKC registerable breeds to compete in AKC Performance and Companion Events. PAL dogs include the many wonderful purebred dogs who may have come from shelters or rescue without AKC registration. (http://www.akc.org/reg/ilpex.cfm)

AKC Canine Partners

AKC Canine Partners is the AKC Program that enrolls mixed breed dogs. AKC Canine Partners is also for purebred dogs of breeds that are not AKC registerable (such as some purebreds from other countries). Hybrid dogs such as the "doodles" are enrolled through AKC Canine Partners.

By enrolling in either PAL or AKC Canine Partners, your dog will receive a number that identifies your dog's record at AKC. When you compete in activities, using this number, your dog's titles are added to a title record. For information on AKC Canine Partners, see: http://www.akc.org/mixedbreeds/index.cfm

Rally

In Rally, you'll enter the ring with your dog. The instructor or judge will explain the course to you and answer any of your questions. Then, the judge will give you the instruction to begin the course. You and your dog will move at your own pace through a series of signs that designate the exercises to be performed. You will be allowed to communicate with your dog throughout the course by talking, clapping, and providing praise. Examples of directions on Rally signs include "Stop and Down," "Moving Down and Walk Around Dog" and "90-degree Pivot Right."

Obedience

Obedience moves beyond the training your dog had in CGC, and it further develops skills in terms of reliability. Obedience provides the training that will give you a dog who is a joy to live with, and it lays the foundation for other canine sports. AKC obedience clubs across the country can help you train your dog to be a better family pet or to compete in obedience competitions.

AKC obedience has different levels for training and competition. In the beginning, you can earn titles that involve exercises done on-leash; in advanced obedience competition, the training wheels come off and your dog is required to work off leash and respond to hand signals.

Agility

You might have seen dogs competing in agility on television. If you did, they were probably on the sports channel, right where great athletes should be. Agility is the fast-paced activity where dogs and their handlers run at top speed around an obstacle course. Some of the equipment includes tunnels, tire jumps, weave poles, the A-frame, and the seesaw. In agility competition, you and your dog will be judged on both speed and accuracy Agility is an excellent form of exercise (for both you and your dog!) and it is often recommended by trainers as a confidence builder for shy, timid dogs.

In addition to Rally, Obedience and Agility, the most common activities for CGC graduates, there are many other exciting training and competition possibilities at AKC.

Conformation

There are more than 160 AKC breeds and varieties of breeds that can compete in AKC conformation dog shows. In these shows, the emphasis lies on the dog's physical structure. In conformation dog shows, the judge decides how closely the dog compares to that judge's mental image of the perfect dog as described in the breed's written standard.

In conformation, dogs compete for points toward their championships. It takes fifteen points to become a champion of record, and the points must be won under at least three different judges.

Dogs in conformation shows may not be spayed or neutered. The purpose of conformation competition is to improve purebred dogs by identifying those that are quality representatives of their breeds and thus desirable for breeding. AKC supports the spaying or neutering of all pet dogs.

Junior Showmanship

Junior Showmanship is the AKC activity that teaches young people between the ages of nine and eighteen how to show dogs, care for and groom them, and develop good sportsmanship. In Junior Showmanship, the skills of the handler are what is being judged, not the dog. Juniors may also complete with their dogs in companion events (such as obedience and agility) and performance events (such as lure coursing and earth dog events, those events designed for certain breeds). There is no minimum age for Juniors are competing in companion events.

Tracking

If you've seen a dog (in real life or television) being used to track a person who is lost in the woods, you've seen a tracking dog. AKC tracking teaches dogs to track and follow human scent. The three titles that can be earned in AKC tracking include Tracking Dog (TD), in which the dog must follow a track from 440 to 500 yards long with three to five changes of direction; Tracking Dog Excellent (TDX) in which the dog must complete a track that is three to five hours old, 800 to 1000 yards long, and has seven changes of direction; and Variable Surface Tracking (VST) which is urban tracking. In VST, dogs track over variable surfaces (such as a parking lot, around a building, and down an alley) in the community. Finally, dogs that earn all three tracking titles earn the title of Champion Tracker (CT).

Performance events

The AKC's performance events showcase purebred dogs in the jobs that their breeds were originally bred to do. Earthdog tests, herding, lure coursing, coonhound tests, field trials, and hunting tests are the events that make up the AKC's performance events. Basset Hounds and Dachshunds can enter field trials. Beagles, retrievers, pointing breeds, and spaniels can participate in field trials and hunting tests.

So thank you for your interest in AKC S.T.A.R. Puppy. We hope that after you train your puppy to be a S.T.A.R., we'll see you and your dog soon at other AKC events.

Conclusion

Do you recognize the dog in this photograph? Take a close look—
you've seen him before.

Effortlessly sailing over a jump in an advanced agility exercise, this is "Tweed," who is owned, loved and trained by Chris Miele. Still not making the connection? This picture shows Tweed in his adult form. He is all grown up in this agility photograph, but he is the puppy on the cover of this book.

Tweed was the very first puppy to pass the AKC S.T.A.R. Puppy test. It was pure coincidence and our extremely good fortune that he happened to be extraordinarily photogenic. Sitting up straight and looking right into the camera, this little pup on our cover seemed so confident and proud.

After AKC S.T.A.R. Puppy, Tweed went on to earn the AKC Canine Good Citizen award. Then, he started training and participating in other events including conformation, rally, and agility.

For Tweed and his owner, training didn't end with AKC S.T.A.R. Puppy—it was just the beginning, and this is exactly the effect that we hoped AKC S.T.A.R. Puppy would have on puppies and their owners.

We hope that you and your puppy will follow in Tweed's paw prints by earning the AKC S.T.A.R. Puppy award as the very first step in a lifetime of training, fun, and building a bond that will last forever.

Index

Selected Titles From Dogwise Publishing
www.dogwise.com 1-800-776-2665

BEHAVIOR & TRAINING

Barking. The Sound of a Language. Turid Rugaas

Bringing Light to Shadow. A Dog Trainer's Diary. Pam Dennison

Canine Behavior. A Photo Illustrated Handbook. Barbara Handelman

Canine Body Language. A Photographic Guide to the Native Language of Dogs. Brenda Aloff

Chill Out Fido! How to Calm Your Dog. Nan Arthur

Do Over Dogs. Give Your Dog a Second Chance for a First Class Life. Pat Miller

Dogs are from Neptune. Jean Donaldson

Oh Behave! Dogs from Pavlov to Premack to Pinker. Jean Donaldson

On Talking Terms with Dogs. Calming Signals, 2nd edition. Turid Rugaas

Play With Your Dog. Pat Miller

Positive Perspectives. Love Your Dog, Train Your Dog. Pat Miller

Positive Perspectives 2. Know Your Dog, Train Your Dog. Pat Miller

Stress in Dogs. Martina Scholz & Clarissa von Reinhardt

Tales of Two Species. Essays on Loving and Living With Dogs. Patricia McConnell

When Pigs Fly. Train Your Impossible Dog. Jane Killion

HEALTH & ANATOMY, SHOWING

An Eye for a Dog. Illustrated Guide to Judging Purebred Dogs. Robert Cole

Another Piece of the Puzzle. Pat Hastings

Canine Massage. A Complete Reference Manual. Jean-Pierre Hourdebaigt

The Canine Thyroid Epidemic. W. Jean Dodds and Diana Laverdure

Dog Show Judging. The Good, the Bad, and the Ugly. Chris Walkowicz

The Healthy Way to Stretch Your Dog. A Physical Therapy Approach. Sasha Foster and Ashley Foster

It's a Dog Not a Toaster. Finding Your Fun in Competitive Obedience. Diana Kerew

K-9 Structure and Terminology. Edward Gilbert, Jr. and Thelma Brown

Tricks of the Trade. From Best of Intentions to Best in Show, Rev. Ed. Pat Hastings

Work Wonders. Feed Your Dog Raw Meaty Bones. Tom Lonsdale

Dogwise.com is your complete source for dog books on the web! 2,000+ titles, fast shipping, and excellent customer service.